THE
ONE-EYED MAN
IS KING

THE
ONE-EYED MAN
IS KING

A Story of Winning

Gordon Graham

With editorial assistance by Veronica Patterson

JOHNSON PUBLISHING COMPANY, INC.
Loveland, Colorado USA

Art Direction and cover design by Raymond L. Mickelic
Cover illustration by Kristina Mickelic

This book is dedicated to my family —
   Janie: who brought me love and shared
   her strength with me when I needed it
   most.
   Tami: who taught me trust as a little girl,
   faith as a teenager and respect as a young
   woman.
   Tina: whose unconditional love brightened
   every day.
   Gordy: my son and my partner.

Without their support I might still be
number 28203.

Contents

Acknowledgments

There have been many other people who have been instrumental in the writing of this book. They include bankers, insurance agents, real estate brokers, C.P.A.s, lawyers, military leaders and government personnel; to name them all would be impossible. They have all had one thing in common: the firm belief that change is possible. My sincere gratitude goes to those people who opened doors and brought new insights to me. Greg Barlow, of the State Board of Community Colleges, gave me the first job that utilized my talents and background and helped me see how to stay out of prison. Sam Kelly, then vice president for Minority Affairs at the University of Washington, gave me my first position directly helping convicts prepare to survive in the outside world.

I'd like to express my appreciation to the many wardens and correctional professionals who have given me the opportunity to work in their institutions. My strongest desire as I complete this book is that men and women who are still in prison, still "consumers of correctional services," will find an idea or a technique in these pages that they can put to use in their own lives.

A special thanks to Lou and Diane Tice and to The Pacific Institute for providing the concepts, the opportunities and the faith that made change possible.

Gordon Graham

In Greek mythology, Pygmalion was a sculptor. He sculpted a model of a beautiful lady, and because of Pygmalion's love for the model he created, a miracle occurred. The marble statue was transformed into a real live beautiful lady. This basic concept suggests that in the development of human potential, the way an individual is perceived by those in supervisory, teaching, and leadership positions has a very strong impact on how the individual sees himself or herself.

Eliza Doolittle in *My Fair Lady* suggests, "Being a lady is not so much who you are, but how you're treated!"

Forward:
In the land of the blind . . .

THE ONE-EYED MAN IS KING is the story of a man who practiced dishonesty and perfected it as a way of life until he knew no other way to exist. It is about a man who had no love for himself or humanity. It is the story of a man who changed dramatically from a scared, naive kid to a sophisticated, manipulative convict leader. Ultimately, he progressed through the complex challenge of change to become the founder and president of a national educational and training organization. *THE ONE-EYED MAN IS KING* is the story of my life.

Not so long ago, I was introduced as Gordon Graham, convict #28203, consumer of correctional services. Today, I am introduced as Gordon Graham, author, lecturer, educator, founder and president of the Human Development Training Institute. Change is my business. My life. I am hopeful that living through my experience via the pages of this book, you, the reader, will reach a new awareness of this truth: that change is possible. I know this is so because I am a product of that change!

Not so long ago, I was a "tough kid" from the streets who left home at the age of twelve. I spent my youth scratching, clawing, surviving—eking out an existence with no direction or purpose.

Not so long ago, I was a man who perceived himself and was perceived by others as a "loser," an outcast. A loner who didn't fit into the normal world of friends, family and happiness. A man who had adjusted to a world where stealing, hustling—some form of violence was the only way of life.

For eighteen years my world and my society revolved around prisons and illegal activities. I had been shot. I had escaped from maximum security prisons. I had been involved in hunger strikes, protests, riots—all kinds of manipulations of the system—and eventually I became a leader in the negative world of prisons.

Whenever I was released from prison, I felt out of place, an alien in the outside world. I didn't see change as possible and felt I was destined to die a "con." I had become a product of the prison environment.

In those early years I felt as if God had erred in my construction, as if He had somehow left out a component in my makeup. Deep down inside, I wanted to belong, to be a part of that other world—the world of the white house, picket fence, children, and unselfish love—I knew existed out there somewhere. But I didn't believe that it was possible for me. I truly felt that I could not become an honest, loving person. In my mind, change was not an option.

That is who I was then.

Today, I am a respected leader in my field, a caring father and a loving husband. I am the president of a highly esteemed and reputable corporation, the proud owner of that white house, complete with picket fence.

What was the secret that eluded me for years and made my life difficult and miserable? How did I find that "other" person inside me?

It wasn't a religious revelation: no thunderbolt from heaven, though God, in His infinite wisdom, allowed me to recognize that I had the ability to free the "other" person that lay dormant inside me for many years.

The process of my change involved a myriad of experiences—some traumatic, some involving just the simple acceptance of the truth. The love and trust of a wife and three beautiful children opened new doors for me. People who saw in me the potential for growth and who offered to me the opportunities to develop that potential gave me hope and encouragement. Those people ranged in positions from lawyers to wardens, from bankers to business executives, and from real estate brokers to military leaders. They all gave me a chance. They saw in me what I could be, not what I had been.

For the past ten years, these people have encouraged me to write a book about my experience in prison and the important changes that occurred in my life. I kept hesitating because so many books had already been written on the life that encompasses the world of prisons. Most of these books are authored by former inmates or former prison officials, some by renowned sociologists. These books have suggested that people in prison are poor misguided individuals who, given love and understanding, will mend their evil ways. Or they suggest that all men and women in prison are corrupt, incorrigible, basically no good, and will never change. These people subscribe to the theory, "lock them up and throw away the key." I did not want to support either opinion.

There have been books written on the brutality and inhumanity propagated by prison officials. There have been books written by ex-convicts which support the adage, "once a criminal, always a criminal." There have been thousands of words written about violent offenders of society's rules being transformed into productive members of that same society. Two things most of these books have had in common were a personal bias for or against the prison system and a "how-to" section describing what was wrong and how to go about changing that wrong. I did not want to participate in any such judgements.

The causes and effects of crime and punishment have been analyzed and scrutinized through magnifying and/or rose-colored glasses by criminologists, sociologists and even singers, since time began.

Why write another book about prison life, I asked myself. I didn't want to be another ex-convict writing about the gory details of prison life. I did not want to castigate prison officials, prison personnel nor the society behind them. I didn't have an ax to grind with anyone. I did what I did and no one else is to blame.

So why write another book about prisons?

This book is not about prisons; it is about taking control of one's own destiny.

This book is about change.

It is a personal testimony that change is possible, that each individual has the potential and the option to change and become a productive, contributing member of society, no matter what his or her past may have been.

This book deals with the process of change and the deep emotional crisis that change brings about. It reveals how change can be beautiful and painful. How it can occur as a result of environmental conditions and spiritual evolution. How change can be easy. How it can be difficult. Most importantly, how change can become a reality for all who seek it.

The responsibility for change is in our own hands. Freedom is not just being out of prison. Many people are in private prisons they have created within their minds. They maintain attitudes that foster unhappiness for themselves and others. They stay in jobs they don't enjoy and remain in relationships that are unhealthy. Often people possess negative self-images that are harmful to themselves and others. All of these are prisons in a different sense, but prisons just the same.

Freedom can be obtained by accepting ourselves for who we are and recognizing that each of us has the choice of changing for the better.

Freedom isn't free. There is a price we all must pay. The price may be different for each of us, but these factors are constant: 1) We must see that change is possible. 2) We must accept responsibility for our own actions. 3) We all must share our love and strengths with those who may not be as strong.

I hope that this book contributes, in some way, to these basic "truths" and that those who read and understand will come away with new strength and a sense of purpose.

This book is not about prisons, escapes, riots, or hard times. It is about the change that occurred in one man. It highlights the events, the environments, the people and the experiences that have made that change possible. Every incident in the book is true.

As you, the reader, journey with me through this complex, sometimes frightening, sometimes funny series of personal events, keep in mind that I do not try to suggest I have all the answers, if any at all. Some sections express my own philosophies and opinions developed over years of constant contact with our criminal justice system, first as a consumer, then as an administrator, and, for the past eight years, as an educator. What I learned during those years, I want to pass on: you do not have to be the way you are if you are unhappy with yourself. You can be free of the opinions of others. You need not live up to the expectations of those opinions. You can control your own destiny. The choice is up to you.

In the land of the blind, THE ONE-EYED MAN IS KING; in a world where people refuse to see that change is possible, the visionary is seen as a threat. If you have the kind of courage and commitment it takes to produce change, you are only a stone's throw from claiming the kingdom of inner peace and prosperity that is yours for the taking.

Gordon Graham

May 1982
Bellevue, Washington

Prologue

The windows at the back of the cell blocks were now filled with bricks and mortar, but otherwise Monroe still looked the same after twenty-five years. I thought of the violent night of my arrival when I had wanted to crash through those windows and escape.

Monroe Reformatory—I'd always felt a certain resentment at the term "reformatory." I'd taught seminars in some of the toughest penitentiaries in the country—Leavenworth, Folsom, San Quentin, Walla Walla—Monroe was not a reformatory. It equalled most prisons when it came to hard time, violence and inmate unrest. A reformatory makes one think of a reform school. Monroe had always housed some of Washington State's most difficult inmates. It was a breeding ground for the men who walk the big yard at Walla Walla, the state penitentiary.

The stairs leading up to the administration building looked the same as they had that morning when I'd stumbled down them wrapped in chains on my way to Walla Walla. I'd visited Monroe a number of times since that morning, but I still felt a slight fear every time I entered the institution. Blue denim coveralls, greasy fritters, and the Hole were memories that the years hadn't erased.

There were few visible signs of change. Metal detectors had been installed to screen inmates and visitors as they entered the institution. Women now worked as correctional officers and inmates were referred to as residents, but it was still Monroe.

They'd outlawed the Hole, where I'd spent so much time. Inmates now had certain rights. Lawsuits, unheard of when I'd been in Monroe, were now commonplace. But prisons don't change—only the faces in them change.

I'd left Monroe twenty-five years earlier, manacled and chained to nine other convicts for the long ride to Walla Walla, a tough undisciplined young man destined to spend his life in prison. I was back twenty-five years later, president of my own training corporation, a respected educator in the correctional system. But the experiences at Monroe had left an indelible mark on my soul. Monroe had been the beginning of seventeen years behind bars. It had been my training ground. I'd learned about violence, fear, humiliation, pain and manipulation. How many other young men had started in Monroe and had never broken out of the system?

I'd driven to Monroe to visit Tony Gallo, a young heavyweight fighter who was awaiting trial. He reminded me of myself. Tony was what I had been twenty-five years earlier: young, tough, and in trouble. His future could hold the pain and misery of years in prison or he could change—but it would take commitment, new concepts about himself, people with faith in him.

Old memories flooded my mind as I walked up the stairs and entered the institution. The three-piece suit and briefcase gave me the appearance of a business executive or a lawyer, but when I entered Monroe, I felt as though I were back in blue coveralls with my prison number tattooed on my forehead. I could hear the lockboxes and feel the cell doors slam behind me.

1. Monroe Reformatory

The cell block was huge. The catwalks that ran in front of the long rows of cells seemed to go on forever. The air was warm and heavy with a strong, pungent smell of antiseptic. The grey cement floors were still wet with dirty streaks of water from their morning scrubbing. The cells looked like long rows of apple boxes standing on end with grey steel bars across the front, like cages.

We shuffled along the corridor of the cell block, dressed in our state-issued, ill-fitting blue denim outfits. An inmate dressed in form-fitted khakis lounged against the door of the first cell on the tier. He eyed us coldly as we passed by.

"Open 'em up," the guard with us yelled.

The khaki-clad inmate reached over and slowly pulled a long lever, and the narrow, barred doors of the individual cells slid noisily open.

"What's happening?"

"The new fish get in?"

"Any pretty ones?"

"I get first choice."

The voices of unseen faces sounded hollow as they echoed through the huge dungeon-like cell block.

"Okay, let's go!" the guard yelled as he moved down the line of cells. He began to call out names and right after the name, the cell number that was printed over each of the narrow openings.

I was the third name called.

"Graham, 9-A."

I shifted my roll of blankets in my arms and walked slowly into the tiny cubicle. It was narrow. You could stand in the middle of it, hold your arms out, and touch both sides with your fingertips. There was a thin, well-used mattress stretched out on a decrepit army cot against one side of the cell. A small sink with most of the enamel worn away was attached to the back wall next to a toilet stained and chipped from years of use.

You can't even take a shit in private! I thought.

It seemed like a final insult to my dignity.

The only other furnishing was a small wooden stool that now served as a table for the small brown paper bag that held my worldly possessions.

The cell door slid shut behind me with the loud clang of metal against metal.

I felt totally alone. The feeling of loneliness was almost suffocating. I sat down on the cot and rubbed my face with both hands. Silently I cried out, if there's a God, why am I here? I'd never needed so much to believe in a God. This new emotion was a feeling of helplessness, as if I were at the mercy of this stark, monstrous cell block.

The noise of doors banging and discordant voices ricocheting off walls and down the long cavernous cell block became almost unbearable. I covered my ears with my hands and thought, why me? Why? This couldn't be happening to me. Not for a lousy hundred-and-fifty-dollar check that I forged. Damn that judge! Damn that prosecutor! I let that sheriff talk me into pleading guilty and believed him when he told me I wouldn't do more than a year in the reformatory. I went to court and pleaded guilty on all charges. The judge, without even batting an eye, sentenced me to twenty years. Twenty years?

"Yes, son, twenty years, but you probably won't do any more than a year to fifteen months, depending on what the parole board decides."

I had been duped. I was guilty, but I had been duped.

"What's happening, man? Where you from?"

The voice startled me out of my reverie. I turned and the inmate who had opened the cells for us was leaning against the bars at the front of my cell. He had reddish-brown hair and a sickish pale coloring that gave him an ominous appearance, much like a vulture's. His arms were covered with tattoos of naked girls and girls' names that looked like the printing of small children.

"I'm the tier boss," he said, pounding his chest with his thumb. "They call me Red. You want anything, you call me." He seemed to be staring at the brown leather wingtip shoes that I'd bought just before getting busted.

"They'll take your shoes, man. The State will just keep 'em."

"What the hell do I wear?" I said. "This is the only pair of shoes I got, man!"

Quickly he replied, "I can get you a pair of State shoes now. They'll give you some tomorrow, but when they do they'll take those wingtips. I can get them put in my property box, which is a hell of a lot better than the damn State getting 'em."

I thought for a moment and said, "I sure don't want to let the State have 'em. You get me a pair of shoes and you can have these." I pulled off my shoes and slid them between the bars. "I wear an eight-and-a-half E."

He took them, and with a crooked grin, he walked away, saying he'd be back in a minute.

I walked back to the cot and unfolded the two brown army blankets, thin from wear, and spread them on the mattress that reeked with a stale odor of urine. I lay down on the bed. The springs on one side were weak and the mattress nearly touched the floor. I lifted myself off the bed, rolled the mattress back, and saw that all the anchor springs on one side were missing. How the hell am I going to sleep on this son-of-a-bitch! These people don't give a shit about nothing!

An inmate was walking by my cell. I called out to him, "Hey, man, could you ask Red to come down here for a minute?"

A couple of minutes later Red strolled up to the front of my cell. He had a pair of well-worn black oxfords in his hands.

"Here you go," he said. "You can get a new pair when you go to the clothing room in the morning. What else can I do for you?"

I pointed to the cot. "I can't sleep on that. Hell, the springs are gone."

"I can get you some springs, but it'll cost a couple of packs of cigarettes." Suddenly, Red was all business.

"I don't have any cigarettes. Hell, I don't even smoke." I didn't like this.

"You can order them at the commissary if you've got enough money on the books," Red said. A shit-eating grin spread across his face. "Hell, you're new. I'll stand good for you. You got any money?"

"Yeah, I've got a couple hundred dollars," I said. "How do I order?"

"I'll bring you commissary slips on Tuesday." He hurried off and returned shortly with three anchor springs that had long since lost their spring. "Got three of 'em. Only two packs. Usually they'll run you a pack each, but the guy's a friend of mine."

He was glancing around my cell and spotted my brown paper bag lying on the stool. "Hey, man, you got tooth powder?"

"Just some in an envelope that the guards gave me when they checked us in." I started to feel better. Someone was interested in me.

"That shit will rot your gums. I can get you a can of good tooth powder. Cost you two packs, but it'll last you till you get to the commissary in a couple days. I better get you a couple of light bulbs, too." He pointed to the ceiling. "Those burn out in a hurry and the Man doesn't care."

I nodded okay.

Red left and it wasn't too long before he was back carrying a small blue can of tooth powder and two light bulbs still in their package.

"That'll be four packs for the tooth powder and light bulbs. That means you owe me six packs. When you make out your commissary order, I'll tell you what to order me." He hurried off, but not before he made one more offer. "If you want hot water for shaves or instant coffee, I'll bring it to you for two packs a week."

I told him I'd think about it and went over and hooked the springs to my bed and straightened out the blankets. The thought of the place left a dry feeling in my mouth. I decided I'd brush my teeth. I took out the yellow toothbrush they'd given me and the envelope of tooth powder. I went over to the sink and pushed the water button; a brown rusty liquid splashed into the scarred sink. Gradually, it cleared. I dipped my brush under the water and sprinkled some of the powder on the bristles. I began to brush; the taste of the powder was terrible. Hell, I'll use my own that Red brought me. I got out the new blue can of tooth powder, cleaned my toothbrush and covered the bristles generously with the powder. I began to brush again. Aaagh! The taste was putrid. It's the same damn stuff that's in the envelope! That son-of-a-bitch sold me state-issue tooth powder. I felt like a damn fool.

I knocked on the wall of the cell next to me. "Hey, man. Eight-A, are you awake?"

He answered, "Yeah, what you want?"

"Did they take your street shoes?" I dreaded the answer.

"Hell no, you keep them. They just check them for metal and give them back. They issue you work shoes and will give you shoes if you don't have any. What happened, did Red con you?"

My voice was almost shy in its answer. "Yeah, he said they'd take my shoes, so I gave them to him." More forcefully I said, "But I'm going to get 'em back."

Eight-A kind of chuckled. "Hey, man, you gonna be a sucker, be a quiet one. Red belongs to a clique that runs this joint. You want something here, you pay for it. And they'll rat-pack you if you jump one of 'em—you've got to fight 'em all." His voice got more authoritative as he continued. "Just do your own time and don't let them get you in debt. They'll run the race horse interest on you and you'll never get out of debt as long as you're here. Last time I was here a guy borrowed a carton of cigarettes and before he could pay it back, he owed five cartons. He never did get out of debt. That's the way they turn young kids into joint punks. We're going to chow soon, better get ready." I could hear him walk to the back of his cell and turn the water on.

What the hell kind of a place is this, I thought. Shit, I owe that bastard six packs, but I sure as hell ain't gonna pay him. How the hell could I go for something so stupid.

I could hear them beginning to open cell doors for chow. The tier bosses hollering "Chow on E tier" was followed by the loud clanging of cell doors as they opened and closed.

I began to walk up and down my cell . . . four steps one way, turn around, four steps the other way. There was a worn path in the middle of the cell floor where other fish had walked thousands of hours before me. The tier above was being let out for chow. It sounded like a herd of stampeding cattle rushing wildly toward a cliff. The cons were cursing and laughing as they charged toward the front of the cell block. Only one thing ran through my mind as I walked up and down the cell: I'm going to get my shoes from that red-haired son-of-a-bitch as soon as they open these doors.

Then it was A tier. "Okay, fish, let's go. Chow time." Red's voice echoed above the din. The narrow steel door of my cell slid open and I stepped out. The tall, stained-glass windows at the end of the cell block gave the place a cathedral-like appearance. As I glanced up and down the tier, other fish were stumbling out of their cells, some half asleep pulling on their clothes, others peering nervously right and left, looking for someone to follow. I spotted Red at the end of the tier leaning against the lock box, one hand resting on the heavy metal bar that unlocked the cells. Everyone was moving toward the front of the cell block. I fell in line with the others.

We approached the front of the tier where Red was leaning against the bars. I fell out of line and walked over to him. "Hey, man, where are my shoes?" My face felt hot. Anger mixed with humiliation and fear surged through me. "You can keep street shoes in here, and I want them back," I said, staring right into his eyes. I was so close I could smell his stale breath.

"Man, you better get back in line. You gave me those shoes. The Man is watchin' and he'll bust you if you don't keep movin'." He sounded scared.

"I don't give a shit! You better get those shoes or I'm gonna kick your fucking ass all over this cell block!" My voice was rising and others were stopping to listen.

Red turned and started to walk into his cell. I grabbed him by the shoulder and pulled him toward me. "Where are my shoes, man? You son-of-a-bitch, I'm not kidding. I want my shoes, and I ain't paying for no damn joint tooth powder either."

He pushed my face with his left hand and I hit him between the eyes with a straight hard right hand. I felt the bone in his long hooked nose crack from the blow. I followed with a left hook to the chin. He started to fall, but grabbed me and wrestled me to the floor with him. We rolled around punching, kicking, and gouging at each other. The other inmates were milling around, excited by the violence. Suddenly two guards came rushing down the staircase and grabbed me around the neck and pulled me off. Red got in a few free shots while they held me. He was bleeding from the nose, which was turning purple and had a new ninety-degree angle to it. He screamed at me as the guards hustled me off, "I'm gonna get you, you bastard!"

The guards relaxed their hold on my arms and neck as we walked through a hallway into another huge cell block that looked exactly like the one we had just left. As we walked along, inmates stared questioningly through their bars at me.

"Where you goin', man?" they yelled.

"He's goin' to the Hole!" another inmate hollered.

"He just got in a beef with Red. Kicked his ass, too!"

"He's been asking for it," somebody knowingly answered.

The voices came from all over the huge cell block. "Some fish kicked the shit out of Red."

"Who was it?"

"Dunno."

It sounded like I'd done something that a lot of the inmates would have done if they had had the courage. "He's a tough son-of-a-bitch. Knocked Red on his ass with one punch. Did it right in front of the Man. You should have seen Red's face." The anger that was in me was gone now, replaced by fear and anxiety. What was going to happen to me?

2. The Hole

We arrived at the very back of the cell block. A pair of wrinkled and faded blue coveralls lay on the floor next to the wall.

"Okay, strip down," the guard ordered.

I took off my flannel shirt, unbuttoned the bluejeans and stepped out of them. I stood shivering in a baggy pair of olive green army shorts.

"Them too," growled the guard, pointing to the shorts.

I pulled the shorts down and kicked them into the pile with my jeans and shirt. I stood naked against the cell block wall, wondering what next. Inmates up and down the cell block were peering out through the bars of their cells, watching our every move.

"Okay, palms against the wall and spread your legs."

The guard placed his foot between mine and pushed them farther apart. "Raise your left foot. Now your right." He ran his hands through my short-cropped hair.

"Now, bend over and spread your cheeks."

I turned so my ass wasn't facing the cells and bent over, reached back and spread the cheeks of my ass. The guard bent over and looked closely.

"Okay, get these on." He threw the wrinkled coveralls at me. I pulled them on. They were loose and a good six inches too long. I felt the heat of embarrassment and humiliation running through my body like a searing hot liquid. One of the guards unlocked a large steel door in the outside wall of the cell block and pulled it open.

"Let's go," one of them said as they pushed me through the door.

Inside, there were two tiers of six cells, one on top of the other. They took me to one of the cells on the bottom tier and unlocked a huge solid steel door that had a small 6" X 6" opening in the middle of it. The opening had a small steel cover over it that could be opened for feeding. They shoved me inside and slammed the door. I could hear the lock grind as one of them turned the key.

It was dark and quiet. As my eyes adjusted to the darkness, I could see a slab of wood along one side of the cell. On top of it was a threadworn blanket smelling of the ever-present disinfectant. I guess that's the bed, I thought. At the back of the cell was a one-piece toilet/sink combination. That was it! Geezus, this place is worse than the first cell I was in. I wondered what would happen next? I felt like everything and everybody was against me. A bitter loneliness engulfed me. I fought back the tears that were welling up inside me. Geezus, why am I here? I felt totally out of control and at the mercy of this monster that had taken over my life.

There was a Bible lying on the wooden slab. I picked it up and started to leaf through it, but the light was dim, and the pages were so worn with age that I couldn't make out the words. Somehow, the Bible being kept here seemed inconsistent with the bleak inhumanity of the dungeon-like surroundings. My senses became aware of the sounds of other people who were locked up in this isolated and forlorn cell block commonly known and aptly referred to as "the Hole." I walked to the front of the cell and looked through the narrow slits between the bars in the small window-like opening of the cell door. Muffled voices came from the other cells.

"Who came in?"

"Did they lock someone up?"

Another voice asked, "Hey, new man, who are you?"

Another added, "What you get locked up for?"

The steady stream of questions demanded an answer.

"I'm Gordy Graham. I got in a fight and they put me in here," I answered.

"Where you from, man?" The voice sounded like the scraping of footsteps on a gravel road.

"Pennsylvania. I'm new in this state. Got here just before I got busted."

"What are you in the joint for, man?" It was "Gravel" voice again.

"First degree forgery. They gave me twenty years. I got railroaded by a lousy lying sheriff," I replied angrily. "What happens now? How long do I stay in here?" I asked.

"They'll take you to Captain's Court tomorrow morning." Another voice that sounded friendlier had taken over from Gravel voice. "Captain Brady will ask you how you plead, find you guilty, and sentence you to either ten days in the Hole or, because you're new, you might get thirty days of privileges taken away."

"Hell, I got in a fight right in front of the Man. They know I'm guilty," I answered.

"You don't plead guilty to nothin' here, man." Gravel voice was back. "It don't make no difference if they got twenty witnesses, you still plead not guilty."

That didn't make much sense, but I said, "Yeah, man, I know what you mean."

I heard the outer door to the Hole open. The voices and laughter from the outer cell block drifted in and sent a deep sense of loneliness through me.

"Chow time. Get ready for your steak," a sarcastic voice laughingly shouted out, joined by another faceless voice. "Yeah, man, steak and eggs. You'll love it."

A guard with a large round face and thin mustache appeared at the window. He unlocked the small barred opening and stuck a hand through it. "Here you go, one fritter." His hand pushed two slices of bread with what looked like a smashed, discolored hamburger patty through the opening. I reached out and took it from him. I couldn't figure out what it was supposed to be, so I held it up to the dull light that came through the bars. It looked soggy, green and brown and a hodge-podge of other colors. It smelled like stale grease. Geezus, this is garbage. I sure as hell ain't going to eat this shit! I laid the greasy bread and strange looking patty on the slab of wood and looked out through the bars. I could hear the guard on the top tier passing out his odious offerings. Suddenly an angry voice from one of the cells above me snarled, "Fuck you. I don't want it. Stick it in your ass, man. Give it to your mama!" I saw the bread fall to the floor outside my cell.

"That's another ten days!" the guard answered heatedly. "You ain't never goin' to get out of here. I don't give a damn if you starve." I could hear the guard's irate breathing as he came down the stairs.

Jeering voices followed him. "Stick it in your ass, dog!"

"Take it home to your wife. She'll love it!"

"Give it. to the warden. He eats shit!" The guard slammed the door to the Hole as a roar of laughter pursued him out into the outer cell block.

What kind of a place is this? These guys are nuts! I got to get the hell out of here! The sense of fear and helplessness rose up again.

"Hey, Graham, how'd you like the steak?" The incident with the guard didn't seem to bother Gravel voice.

"Man, I ain't going to eat this shit. It's garbage." I made myself sound tough, trying to beat down the fear inside of me.

A voice from above shouted, "Let's flood this son-of-a-bitchin' Hole!" I knew it was the same guy who had cursed the guard.

"They'll just turn the water off, man," a sing-song voice chipped in.

"Don't make any noise. Just fill your sinks and keep flushing your toilets. But we all got to do it, " the insane voice yelled.

As I was to find out a short time later, the one with the insane voice was named Charley. The gravel-voiced one was called "Bull Dog" Brown, and the one who appeared to be enjoying himself was aptly named "Lu Lu" Dodge.

"Okay, let's all start at once," Charley ordered. I could hear water beginning to run and toilets being flushed continuously. Before long, water was falling in a steady stream in front of my cell. "Pick your stuff up off the floor," Lu Lu hollered. "It'll get clear up over your bed if they don't shut it off first."

"Tear up some of your blanket and throw it out in front of your cell so it'll plug up the drains," someone yelled.

Small strips of blanket and what looked like pages from the Bible were thrown from cells onto the floor where they floated to the drain that was imbedded in the very center of the cell block. The water was now running under my door and covering the cement floor. It was cold on my bare feet. I stepped up on the narrow plank that served as my bed. The Bible was lying next to my feet. I picked it up and put it in the sink.

If this water keeps rising, it's going to cover my bed, I thought to myself. This is crazy. Hell, these guys are flooding themselves out and me with them. I felt like screaming to them to stop, but I knew it wouldn't do any good and they'd label me as a chicken.

The water continued to rise and was now beginning to break over the top of the wooden slab. It was getting colder. I perched myself on the sink with my legs drawn up under my chin. It was dry, but the metal edges felt sharp through my thin coveralls.

The cons on the bottom tier started to bitch about the dilemma they had caused. "Hey, man, the water's over my bed!"

"Shit, man, I'm freezing my nuts off!"

"Shut the goddam water off!" The anger and violence was gone from the faceless voices, replaced by cold anguish and chattering despair.

"When it gets a little later, everybody start banging on your doors. It'll wake the guys in the main cell block." Charley's voice hadn't changed. It was still violent, uncompromising.

How can anyone live like this, I wondered. This is senseless. When I get out of here tomorrow, I sure as hell ain't coming back. It was getting late and the Hole was pitch black. The cell was cold and had water over six inches deep on the floor.

"Okay, let's wake 'em up," Charley's irrational voice commanded. The silence was broken by the violent clanging of metal against metal as doors were rattled and kicked by the inmates who were confined in the tiny cell block. As the barrage of noise became more and more intense, I could hear the beginning murmurs of voices coming from the main cell block that was connected to the Hole.

"Shut those bastards up in there."

"Whaaa-the! They're flooding the fucking cell block!"

"Water's comin' into my cell. Man, up! Man, up!"

Their voices were louder now. The banging from the doors in the Hole was now being drowned out by the irritated shouts and the banging of metal against metal, plus the added bedlam of steel doors being rattled with tremendous force. The night was filled with a chaotic fury that bordered on lunacy.

"The Man's comin'. Shut off your water," Gravel voice warned. I could hear the outside door being opened and then the bellowing voice of a guard.

"All right, you assholes, we're shutting off the water in here and if you make any more noise, we'll fill this place with tear gas. You got the whole damn joint awake!"

I could now hear more clearly the inmates in the main cell block hollering and shouting their displeasure.

"Are they gassing them?"

"Who the hell's in there?"

"Shit, man, I gotta work in the morning!"

"Can't you keep those fuckers quiet?"

As quickly as it had started, the din subsided. The guards left and the inmates in the main cell block began to quiet down. The short moment of rebellion was over.

I reached down and pushed the button on the sink. The water caught in the pipes, dripped weakly, and then quit. I wonder what you drink? I hope I don't have to take a shit tonight. My stomach started rumbling, which reminded me that I was hungry. I thought about the food I'd laid on my wooden bed. I rolled the pants legs of my over-sized coveralls up to my knees and stepped down into the cold water. I made my way to the corner where I'd placed the greasy fritter. The water had turned the bread into mush and the thin vegetable patty crumbled in my hands as I tried to pick it up. Now I *really* can't eat this. I'll just have to tough it out until the morning.

I returned to my perch on the sink and rolled the long legs of the coveralls down and wrapped them around my feet. Geezus, I don't know if I can spend the rest of the night on this damn sink. The sides were cutting into my ass. I stood on the edge of the toilet and adjusted the blanket on and around the sink so it would cushion my seat. Better, I thought, as I shifted from one cheek to the other, wishing the morning would get there soon.

The night went on forever. The small cell block was silent now, the stillness broken only by the dripping of water, the muffled sound of coughing and an occasional curse as someone stepped in the cold water. I started thinking of the bizarre events of my first day in prison. The senselessness of it all brought deep painful sobs of self-pity. I felt like praying to God for answers to why I was here and what was going to become of me, but somehow it didn't seem right. Sometimes I believed in Him; sometimes I didn't. But how could a God allow something like this? He must not know, or He wouldn't allow it to happen. He knows everything. We were taught that. When I'm out of this and don't need anything, I'll ask Him.

Hazy streaks of light were beginning to play on the outer walls of the cell block. I had somehow dozed off. It must be morning. I wondered what time it was. I got down from the sink. My ass ached from the sharp metal ridges that had cut into my flesh. The water had receded and only the damp, cold floor and crumbled bits of food remained from the insanity of the night before.

"You awake down there, Gordy?" It was the one called Lu Lu. He sounded as though nothing had happened.

"Yeah, man, I've been in my damn sink all night." I was cold, tired, and hungry.

"You've got to be on the top deck, man. The water runs off the tier onto the bottom floor. If you're up here, your bed stays dry. We flood it all the time and raise hell at night to wake up the guys in the big cell block. Sometimes you can get the whole joint banging their cell doors so loud that the people can hear it downtown." He sounded proud of this accomplishment. He continued, "You'll be going to court in a little while. See if you can score a smoke or two while you're out there. I've got a couple of matches."

"If I come back here? I don't think I will." I sounded sure of myself. I waited for reassurance but none came.

Gravel voice, Bulldog Brown, was awake and in true form. "Somebody wake up that goddam Charley. He raises hell all night and then sleeps all day." He sounded disgusted.

Another voice complained, "Man, they're gonna write us all up for floodin' this son-of-a-bitch, and I was supposed to get out to-day . . ." The voice broke.

I felt sorry for him.

It wasn't too long before the outer door opened. I could hear the guards come into the Hole. They stopped in front of my cell and the key rattled in the lock.

They're letting me out! The elation wiped the tiredness from my body.

"Let's go, Graham. Captain's Court." The guard who spoke had lieutenant's bars on his shirt and wore a hearing aid. He looked like a retiree from an old folks home just putting in his time. The other guard was small, with a potbelly that hung over his belt. His dark-tinted glasses made him look like a fat beetle.

Advice from fellow cons greeted me as I stepped out of my cell.

"Plead not guilty, Graham."

"Don't tell them shit, man."

"Tell the captain to get fucked."

I inhaled deeply and looked around this infamous cell block called the Hole. It had six small cells on the bottom tier, where I was, and six that sat on top of those. The top cells had a catwalk that ran in front of them. I tried to catch a glimpse of just one face to match the voices I heard, but all the door openings were closed. I looked up at the skylight and noticed the broken panes of glass that allowed the cold fall air into the cell block. Boy, I bet this is a cold son-of-a-bitch in the winter.

We walked out the door and down a long tier into an area that separated two huge cell blocks that appeared identical. I recognized the tier where I had first been placed when I came in. Red was leaning back on a stool reading a paperback novel. Anger filled me. That no good son-of-a-bitch got me put in the Hole. I'll fix him when I get back. The guards took me to the bottom of a long narrow steel staircase that ran to the very top of the cell block. A catwalk ran across to the top tier. A number of other inmates lounged against the wall at the foot of the staircase. They must be going to court too, I thought. The others were dressed in bluejeans and shirts. I felt awkward and out of place in the baggy, over-sized overalls.

"You wait here." The lieutenant turned and walked up the stairs to the top, opened a door, and disappeared into what appeared to be the control room. The beetle-like guard sat down on the bottom of the stairs.

"What's happening, Smitty?" one of the inmates asked. The "Beetle" just grunted and pulled out a plug of tobacco, took a huge bite, leaned back contentedly, closed his eyes, and seemed to doze off.

The other inmates were playing a guessing game as to their fate at the hands of the captain. They all seemed to know each other.

"I got busted with some 'pruno' (homemade brew). Had it set up in my 'shitter.' I think someone snitched on me. It was ready to drink. Smelled real good, too." The inmate talking looked like a logger—big, burly, with heavy work boots.

"I got caught with two steaks. Shit, I was taking them to my partner. He missed chow." This one looked like a weasel, thin with a razor-like face and a whiny voice.

A short, stocky black guy asked me what I had been busted for. He seemed friendly. I talked low so no one else could hear and told him about the fight and the night in the Hole.

"Man, you guys sure raised hell down there last night. Woke up the whole damn joint. I couldn't get to sleep at all," he replied.

The door at the top of the steel staircase opened and the lieutenant stepped out. "Okay, you guys, listen up. When your name is called, you come up to the third step from the top and I'll read your charge. You plead guilty or not guilty. The captain will make a decision, and if there's a question of guilt, you'll be called to the full court on Friday. This is the order you'll be called: Larson, Geer, Potts, Graham."

I'm fourth. That's good, I thought. At least I can see what the hell to do.

The captain stepped smartly from the sliding door and out onto the ramp beside the lieutenant. He was a short man, completely bald; he wore dark glasses and what looked like riding boots shined to a glossy finish. His uniform was form-fitted and the light bounced off his shiny captain's bars. I didn't like his looks. I'll bet he's a mean son-of-a-bitch, I thought.

"Larson, let's go," barked the lieutenant. The logger climbed the stairs and stopped three steps from the top. The captain looked down and you could hear him rattle off the charge. "Making pruno in your cell. How do you plead?" You couldn't hear Larson's answer, but the captain seemed to consider his remark, rubbed his bald head, and stated loudly, "Guilty. Ten days in the Hole. Next." Larson came slowly down the stairs. He looked like he wanted to cry but tried to smile and act as though it didn't bother him.

"I can do ten standing on my head," he declared boldly as he passed the con who looked like a weasel.

You might have to do it sitting in your sink, I thought.

The other two went before me and returned with the same luck as Larson. All of a sudden, I didn't feel too well.

"Graham, let's go."

I climbed the cold steel stairs slowly in my bare feet. The baggy, rolled-up coveralls made me feel foolish. I stopped the required three steps below the captain and stared up at him. Up close, his bald head looked like a slick peeled onion. He looks just like one of the Gestapo agents in those thirties and forties movies, I thought.

He looked down at me through those dark glasses. His face was emotionless. "You've been here all of one day and you're in a fight with the tier boss and also involved in flooding the Hole. You're getting a good start." The voice was cold and lifeless. "How do you plead?"

I could hear the advice from Lu Lu and the others still ringing in my ears: never plead guilty! It didn't make any sense.

"Speak up," the lieutenant ordered.

"Guilty of fighting, but I really wasn't involved in flooding the Hole." I don't want to go back to the Hole, I screamed silently.

"Guilty of fighting *and* flooding the Hole." The captain remained expressionless. "Ten days in the Hole on each count. Because you're new, I'm going to run them concurrently. You come back here again and I'll bury you. We know how to deal with you tough guys." He turned to the lieutenant. "Who's next?"

At first I was shocked, then anger took over. I'm a person. Look at me with your eyes, you heartless Gestapo bastard.

"How can you find me guilty without any evidence?" I heard myself say. "I wasn't involved in flooding the fucking Hole. I admit I lost my temper and got in a fight, but that's all." I stood there in baggy overalls, shouting at the captain of the guards.

"Run the sentences consecutively." The voice snapped like a bullwhip. "Twenty days. You'll learn, boy, you'll learn. Take him away."

3. Becoming a "Con"

Those first years in the Monroe Reformatory gradually caused me to adjust to an image that controlled my behavior for the next thirteen years. The Hole, greasy fritters, flooded cell blocks, and tear gas had became an accepted part of my existence. I found that residents preyed upon residents, and the staff members were certainly not there to provide any kind of assistance. Their job was to lock you up and keep you locked up and make sure you followed the rules which were rigged and sometimes seemed ridiculous. I violently opposed convict cliques and the regimented routine of prison life. Consequently, I was in strife constantly with other cons, placed in the Hole time after time, and labelled a troublemaker by the guards.

The short fifteen-month sentence the parole board had given me for forgery had been parlayed into over four years. My continuous fighting and lack of manipulative skills had caused the administration to classify me as a rebel, but to the inmates I was a "good convict"—someone you didn't mess with, who would fight at the slightest provocation, and who wouldn't take shit from the guards. Inmates began to give me "my space" and a grudging respect. Two of the major factors in how you are treated in prison are your physical toughness and your willingness to back your words with actions. I would not allow myself to be pushed around by anyone. A loose-knit group of inmates began to form around me. They were inmates who were disillusioned with bullies and gangs, who basically cared about other people. A subtle power shift took place. The strength that holds gangs together is generally two or three tough inmates who control by fear. As the leaders are transferred or paroled, the weaker inmates begin to look elsewhere for protection.

There was also at this time an administrative power struggle going on between "Onion Head," the Gestapo-like captain, and an associate warden. The captain supported the "con boss" idea, which meant that inmates were in control of all the decisions inside the walls. These con bosses decided where you would work, gave out cell assignments, dictated whether you played on one of the athletic teams, and controlled the lock boxes in the cell blocks that determined whether you could get in or out of your cell. Inmates were even in charge of the periodic head counts that assured everyone was still in prison where he belonged.

Inmate leaders backed the captain because they had control of these con boss positions. This caused a growing discontent inside the prison. Inmates were being forced to pay rent to live on certain tiers. Everything had a price tag. It could cost from two to ten cartons of cigarettes for a decent job. The weaker inmates were forced to pay for protection or they were physically abused. Many of the young, inexperienced inmates were coerced into homosexual affairs by fear and the inability to cope with the more sophisticated, smooth-talking convicts.

The associate warden believed the cons had too much power. He was against the con-boss system and wanted to eliminate it totally. The captain and the associate warden's personal conflict was creating unrest in all aspects of the prison life. The warden was caught in the middle. He was from the old school of letting his subordinates work out their problems among themselves until something happened that warranted his personal attention.

The convict leaders had left me alone after a series of fights and fruitless attempts to scare me into submission. The fear of being ganged-up on or stabbed was always there, but I learned to hide it behind anger and hostility. Fighting was an almost daily occurrence during my first years in prison. I would get released from the Hole for one altercation, and before the day was over, I'd be back in it for another.

After my first twenty-day experience in the Hole, I learned to request a cell on the top tier to avoid the discomfort caused by the frequent floodings. As I became more familiar with the regulars, those who always seemed to be in the Hole with me, I was able to convince them that flooding ourselves out didn't really make sense. Charley would never accept the idea, but as time went on, he had more difficulty getting the other cons to join his insane outbursts of anger. The violent banging of doors and general hell-raising was still accepted because this created an uproar among the three hundred inmates in the huge cell block just outside the Hole. It was a way to scream at the Man and the rest of the prison population: "We're still here, you son-of-a-bitches!"

After being in the Hole many times, I developed unique survival techniques almost without conscious awareness. I learned that if you allowed the vegetable patty from your daily ration to sit for a while, it became much easier to eat. You just ate the two slices of bread for a couple of days and put the fritter in the corner to age. Then, after two days, it became semi-edible. You ate one and you always had one in the aging process. Lu Lu Dodge, who proudly held the joint record of twenty-six times in the Hole, told me how to make a hammock from the single blanket each inmate was allowed. You took one corner and tied it to the steel bars in the cell door and you tied the other corner to the steel rod on the side of the toilet that was designed to hold the sandpaper-like tissue provided in each cell. Then you could carefully place your body in the middle of the folded blanket and it became a makeshift hammock. When I was wrapped in this cocoon-like position, I could touch the sides of the cell with my hands and swing slowly back and forth for hours, searching the tattered yellow-paged Bible for answers to my existence.

The endless monotony was broken occasionally by games of

"twenty questions" that generally ended in accusations of cheating and threats to kick someone's ass "when I get outa the Hole." Stories of Cadillacs, shapely blondes, and capers that had brought the storyteller thousands of dollars filled the long hours. My first degree forgery conviction for a hundred and fifty dollars didn't stand up too well, so it became a massive payroll check operation; and my Pontiac became a brand new Bonneville. The more money you had stolen and the more anti-social your behavior was, the more prestige was bestowed upon you. By day you tried to convince the Man you were honest and could make it outside, but at night you became involved in the wild fantasies that included stealing, drugs and orgies.

4. The Riot

It was a warm day in August. I had just gotten out of the Hole after doing ten days for leaping over a steam table after an inmate who had placed jello on top of my mashed potatoes and gravy. It was an accepted practice to mess with a guy's food if he opposed the cliques. The clique members worked behind the steam tables and would hand out small portions of food or slop the food on the tray so it mixed together. The inmates who were in prison for rape or child molesting lived with this humiliation daily. They generally accepted the degradation without protest for fear of bodily harm.

I was in the yard exercising when an inmate named Jeff, who had been in the Hole with me a couple of times, joined me in my workout of jumping rope and shadow boxing.

"Hey, man, you want to get out of here?" His voice was a whisper.

The asinine question prompted me to regard him warily as I answered, "Are you kidding! Sure I want out, doesn't everyone? But I still got over a year to do." I continued to move around, throwing punches at imaginary opponents.

"Some of us are planning to escape and wondered if you want to join us." Jeff sounded excited and sincere.

There was always someone talking about escape and I didn't pay much attention to him other than to ask, "How the hell are you going to get out of here?"

"We got some bolt cutters, and while some guys create a diversion in the big yard, we're gonna cut our way through the window at the back of the new block." His voice began to rise in hopeful anticipation but dropped as a couple of other inmates strolled by. "Hell, man, that puts us right out on the lawn where the guard towers can't see, and from there it's only a half mile to town. We'll steal a car and be in Seattle before they know we're gone."

It sounded like it might work. I stopped my exercising and looked him in the eye. "What kind of diversion?"

"A group of guys are going to refuse to come in from the yard tomorrow night. When they call yard-in, they're gonna create a hell of a racket and charge the brick plant. We've got the bars about halfway cut and it won't take but a couple of minutes to knock them out with the bolt cutters. The noise from the yard will have all the guards at the front of the cell block and they won't hear us over the racket."

My stomach began to tingle at just the idea of getting out. "It might work. How many guys are going?"

He named four other inmates. One was Red, the guy who had beaten me out of my shoes when I first came to the joint. He had been out of prison and was back for violating parole. I had gotten my shoes back. They just showed up in my cell one day, but I'd never spoken to Red since that first fight. I knew he'd instigated a lot of the shit I'd been through but didn't have the guts to do anything himself.

"Count me out, man. I don't like Red. He's tied up with the clique that works for that son-of-a-bitch Captain Brady. Hell, they might be waiting outside to blow us away."

"Hey, man, the guy's changed," Jeff responded. "He's the one who smuggled the bolt cutters from the metal shop. The guy got married when he was out last time. His old lady has been messing around, and she's gonna leave him. He's the one who asked me to talk to you. He says he was wrong on that shoe deal and doesn't have any bad feelings toward you."

The thought of freedom and all the negative shit that was happening in the joint tempted me. "Sure, I want out. This place is driving me crazy. Where you meeting tomorrow?"

"We're gonna meet in the mess hall," Jeff said. "Red will have the bolt cutters planted in the cell block. Three of us will stay in from the yard tomorrow night, and three will go out and come in when they call early yard-in. That way, we won't all be hanging around the new block and get the guards suspicious."

We moved across the dry, dusty baseball field as we talked. The evening shadows were beginning to slide across the prison yard. Small clusters of inmates slowly moved toward the stark brown cell blocks that were waiting to lock them away in the confines of their steel bowels.

We walked through the gate in the fence that separated the prison yard from the cell blocks. I looked up. The sun bounced brightly off the tops of the beautiful green hills that rose in the distance beyond the red brick wall. Man, I'd like to be out. The desire to be free was powerful.

"Count me in, man," I said. This time there was no hesitation. "I'll see you tomorrow."

We parted and I re-entered the cell block with its familiar wave of noise. The clanging of steel doors and voices yelling last minute obscenities bounced against my brain. I walked down the narrow cat-walk to my cell on the third tier, responding automatically to the greetings of fellow inmates. My mind raced with excitement at the prospect of escape.

The next day seemed to drag on forever. I kept looking for a clock and asking for the time every five minutes. When the call of yard-out sounded, it signalled the beginning of the evening exercise period. I hurried down the tier. The excitement was building inside of me as I went through the gate into the yard looking for Jeff.

The prison yard was hot. The blazing August sun was moving westward, creating a narrow shadow along the base of the twenty-foot wall. Inmates were moving toward the thin slice of shade to escape the late afternoon heat. A pick-up game of baseball was being organized, and a couple of guys were throwing a football back and forth. I could see the heat waves dancing on the flat roof of the prison cannery. The two-story building that housed the education department and the auto shop created a lengthening shadow that was starting to climb the wall of the powerhouse. The whole scene looked like a surrealistic painting where forms and colors blend together, then separate and form again in another part of the frame.

The dreaded brick plant, where many of the inmates worked during the day, sat off to the side. It was quiet now, resting from another day of spewing forth its fierce heat. For most, working in the brick plant was a form of punishment. The clay pit that was covered by a long wooden shed had broken the spirit of more than one malcontent. A row of evenly stacked red bricks formed a wall between the inmates in the yard and the huge wooden structure. I thought of the days I had pushed the wheelbarrow full of heavy clay up and down the narrow catwalk until my back ached and my legs felt like jelly.

There were about three hundred inmates in the yard. A baseball game was in full swing. Inmates were walking the yard, heads down, brown shoulders hunched against the heat. A game of touch football had created a small group of spectators at the far end of the yard. A number of convicts were moving through the yard spreading the word. "When they call yard-in, refuse and attack the brick plant."

You could feel the tension building as the inmates began to drop out of the games and join the small groups that were beginning to cluster around the yard. I was walking by myself, wondering where Jeff was, when he and another con named Dave fell in beside me.

"You ready, man?" Jeff asked in a tight, tense voice. His short, powerful body, built up over the years from pumping weights, was shirtless and glistened with perspiration.

"I'm ready," I said. "When's it going down?"

"They're doing a good job of organizing," Dave said, pointing around the yard with his eyes. He was an older guy who did his own time, and nobody bothered him. Over the years we'd spent some time talking. I knew he had a wife and two sons. He'd gotten busted for stealing some copper wire and had pleaded guilty to grand larceny. Dave was moody and bitter over the five-year sentence the parole board had given him.

I glanced around the yard and noticed all activity had stopped. The inmates were moving slowly en masse across the yard toward the brick mill. I could feel the explosive atmosphere all around me.

The guards had now come out of their towers on the prison wall and were leaning over the rail, looking down on the yard, their rifles nestled in the crooks of their arms. One old guard in the yard was moving around trying to break up the groups of milling inmates.

"Shit, man, what the hell's going on?" I asked. "They ain't supposed to start nothing until *after* early yard-in!" I looked at Jeff. His face was drawn with tension.

"I don't know, but if the bastards don't break it up, they're gonna clear the yard." His words seemed to trigger the order.

The guard's voice came over the P.A. system. "Yard-In, everybody out of the yard. Let's go." His voice crackled with static.

"Fuck you," an inmate's voice screamed. "Let's get the brick plant."

A small group of inmates began to run toward the long wooden structure that had punished so many over the years. They were yelling encouragement to others as they ran.

"Get it."

"Tear the bastard down!"

"Burn it!"

Inmates began to run wildly across the yard. Dust billowed in the air. There was no organization—everyone was going helter-skelter. The years of anger and frustration had exploded like a pressure cooker that builds beyond the capabilities of the container. Someone shouted to get the cannery and the stream of bodies split into two rampaging rivers of humanity.

I found myself caught up in the madness, and I too started running across the prison yard toward the powerhouse. The pent-up anger had also erupted inside of me. I wanted to strike out at this monster that had caused me so much pain and misery.

The one old guard was trying to restore order. He was waving his arms, frantically trying to halt the mass of uncontrollable rage that was all around him. An inmate running beside me dropped his shoulder and drove it into the guard's chest. Out of the corner of my eye, I could see him sprawled in the dust.

Smoke was pouring from the brick mill. The air was filled with dust, smoke, explosions, and the insane screams of the rioting inmates. Some were striking out wildly at wood and bricks as though they were human.

I entered the door of the powerhouse. There was a small group of inmates violently attacking the walls of the building. One had a baseball bat and was beating on a picture that was painted on the cement wall. The thought of escape was lost in this totally overpowering feeling of bedlam and destruction.

I moved from the powerhouse to the laundry, where guys were wrecking machinery with anything they could get their hands on and dumping everything in sight onto the floor. In the small dry-cleaning shop in front of the laundry, a group of cons was emptying cans of cleaning fluid on clothes, presses and walls. Animalistic screams of "Burn it down! Burn it down!" were coming from an inmate named Joe. I could see the wild and frantic look in his eyes as he was trying to strike a match to ignite the fluid that covered everything.

"Hold it, man, you'll trap everybody in here," I hollered at him. I grabbed his arm and screamed at the other inmates to get out before the place exploded.

"Let me go, you bastard. I'm going to burn this fucking place to the ground," he screamed in my ear as we fought. I spotted a guy I knew and yelled to him to get everyone out the back or they'd be trapped and burnt to cinders.

When everyone was out, I released Joe and ran from the building. Moments later, a burst of flame exploded as the cleaning fluid ignited. It was as if everyone had been suddenly injected with a shot of instant insanity. The wood structure that had housed the brick plant was gone. Only a charred shell remained. Multi-colored flames and orange smoke were shooting up into the night skies. The cannery, auto shop, and the large two-story school building were all aflame, turning the night into a raging inferno. Only the powerhouse and a small wooden building that housed the athletic equipment had been spared.

Inmates were now beginning to turn their attention to the prison walls, shouting obscenities at the guards who formed a grey silhouette on the metal catwalks that circled the outside of the wall. They had been joined by state police and local law enforcement people from the surrounding communities. The flames of the burning structures cast shimmering reflections from the gun barrels that moved slowly from side to side like serpents looking for a place to strike.

Cons were shouting and dancing, arms waving wildly, in savage celebration of what they had done. The background of smoke and flames gave the whole scene an eerie and nightmarish appearance.

Someone would suddenly break from the group and run toward the wall to hurl rocks, sticks, and debris at the guards, oblivious to the menacing gun barrels. Then he would turn and dash back to the main body of inmates for protection.

One inmate came running from the small building that served as an athletic shack, his arms loaded with boxes of baseballs. "C'mon, let's knock that tower out," he yelled as he ran toward a corner guard tower. Other inmates were now running to the stacks of red bricks, grabbing armloads and rushing back to join the insane attack on the tower.

Inmates had begun to reassemble after their rampaging anger had been satisfied. There was no cover in the yard and I thought to myself, if they start shooting, this is going to turn into a blood bath.

The voice could hardly be heard over the shouting that filled the yard. "Get back or we'll shoot."

The Man had had enough.

The inmates became still for a moment, then someone shouted the challenge of illogical men everywhere, "Fuck you!" More obscenities were hurled and the jeering and throwing of objects continued.

The crack of a rifle shot exploded from the wall like God stepping upon a giant dry twig.

The yard froze in silence.

"They're shooting blanks," one inmate yelled mockingly.

Rifle shots began to come from other parts of the wall and an inmate screamed in disbelief, "I'm hit. They shot me!"

A con behind me hollered out, "Blanks, my ass! They're shooting real bullets! Get down!"

Hell suddenly raged from the wall and the night air filled with the whine of bullets and the screams of panic-stricken men. Pandemonium broke loose as bodies ran in every direction, frantically searching for cover. The thud of tear gas pellets was followed by their familiar pungent smell, blended with dust and smoke.

I found cover behind a pile of bricks. Others dove to the ground beside me. They were beginning to stack on top of each other in a desperate attempt to escape the hail of bullets that rained down upon us. Some tried to dig holes in the ground with their hands in order to avoid getting hit. I could hear the angry whine of bullets as they slapped at the bricks, then ricocheted off into the night.

"I'm hit," a con beside me screamed in agony. "I can't see!"

I rolled over to help him. His face was a mass of blood. A bullet had ripped across his face, leaving a deep gash where his eyes had been.

"I'm blind! I can't see! Oh God!" he moaned in pain.

Another inmate to my left cried out, "We've got a dead one here!"

The savagery continued.

"Somebody give me a white T-shirt," I yelled. I grabbed the shirt and waved it wildly in the air. "Stop shooting! We've got a dead man here and a guy who's been blinded," I screamed as loudly as I could.

"Let the bastards die!" a voice from the wall shouted back, and the madness continued.

Then as suddenly as it had started, it ended.

The silence was broken only by the screams and sobs of pain from wounded inmates.

Over the P.A. System a voice ordered, "All right, everybody, move out to the infield. Put your hands on your heads and sit down.'' I could see inmates beginning to stand slowly and move silently toward the baseball diamond.

"What about the guys who've been shot," I yelled.

"We'll send stretchers for them," the unsympathetic voice answered. "The rest of you get your asses on the ballfield—now!''

I lay there listening to the gulping sobs of pain that came from the inmate who had been blinded. I knew him slightly. He never caused trouble and just happened to be in the yard when the riot erupted.

I stood. My body was drained. I felt as though something had taken control of me during the hours of rioting. The shock at what had occurred left me empty and bewildered.

Insanity is contagious. Anybody can catch it. The thousands of rounds fired into the yard at unarmed human beings were as senseless and insane as the violence and destruction caused by the inmates.

I joined the mass of other dazed convicts jammed together on the dusty infield. The periodic explosions from the burning building sent showers of sparks into the darkness of the warm night—reminders of the senseless acts of destruction.

We spent two days on the infield, shivering together at night and sweltering under the heat of the hot August days. The wounded were moved to the prison hospital and the inmate who had been shot to death was released to be buried at home. The inmates who stayed inside the cell blocks also had joined in the carnage. They had burned and ripped away the inside of the prison in support of the violence in the yard. The escape had never taken place. In the fury of the riot, the years of pent-up anger and frustration had replaced the careful planning for freedom.

At noon on the third day, we were ordered to strip naked and were searched thoroughly. Then, with a state patrolman on each side of us, we were marched back to the cell blocks. Burned mattresses, ripped furniture and broken glass covered the cell block floors.

Inmates pressed against the bars of their cells, trying to see what was happening and to whom. Some hollered my name and others just wanted to make contact with someone from the yard.

"How you doing, Gordy?"

"Who got killed?"

"How many guys got shot?"

"You okay, man?"

"We tore this son-of-a-bitch up, didn't we, baby?"

When we entered the Hole, the familiar voice of Lu Lu called out, "Who'd they bring in? What the hell's going on out there?"

I was too exhausted to answer him. I sank down on the hard wood slab and covered my face. I closed my eyes, trying to shut out the past few days. But the pictures kept flashing across my mind . . . blood streaming from Andy's eyes, his screams ripping at my guts . . . the dead inmate's head lying on a pile of hard red bricks . . . the old guard struggling in the dust . . . flames, smoke, bullets, the incessant noise of terror all around me . . . until exhaustion finally released me from it all.

My reputation as a troublemaker plus my visibility during the latter stages of the riot caused the administration to tab me as one of the ringleaders. Actually the riot had occurred spontaneously, without planning or leadership. The planned escape and the necessity to cover it contributed to the riot, but the real cause was the years of pent-up anger and frustration in the inmates. There were no ringleaders, but someone has to pay.

5. Solitary

Twenty of us were singled out as ringleaders. Most were hastily transferred to the state penitentiary at Walla Walla. I was placed in my familiar quarters in the Hole with a sentence of 365 days in isolation.

The days ran together, separated only by daylight and darkness. They wore on into weeks until finally time lost meaning. Sounds became increasingly familiar. When I first entered the Hole, the sound of a key being inserted into a door lock sent the adrenalin racing through my veins. I imagined that the Man had discovered a mistake in my sentence and that I would be released. But gradually I lost hope and accepted my fate. Soon the sounds of keys turning and doors opening didn't get through my awareness. I existed in a fog-like world.

The noise of inmates returning to their cells, metal clanging against metal as doors opened and closed in the outer cell block, gave assurance that the world still was going on out there somewhere.

The muffled sounds of voices drifted into the grey dingy Hole. Where was God in all this madness? I prayed that He would not allow me to die in the stinking Hole. I knew that asking more would be unfair.

Twenty-four hours a day, the routine became almost unbearable. The nights were long. The darkness brought with it quiet sobs from men who had not yet adjusted to the loneliness of it all. But somehow the endless blackness made way for tomorrow and then the first streaks of dawn. Daylight brought a faint glimmer of hope that something, anything, might happen.

Inmates began moving about in their cells. The smallest noise was magnified in the tiny cell block. I could hear an inmate urinate followed by the loud flushing of a toilet. In the background I heard noises of heavy breathing and the slap of bare feet on the cement floor as exercise routines were carried out.

Then the questions began, assuring me and my fellow inmates that we were not alone.

"You awake Lu Lu?"

"I think I'm getting out today."

"When they gonna bring those fritters?"

"What time is it?"

"Trade you my bread for your fritter."

"I'm starved."

Responses were ignored. They really didn't matter. It was the questions themselves that mattered; they put you in contact with some kind of reality. I covered my ears. I had heard the same questions over and over. The inmates changed, but the conversation and the misery went on.

I wanted to scream, "Shut up, you bastards." I endured. When it was 9:00 a.m. and the key turned in the outer cell, I knew it was fritter time. I could hear the guard moving through the cell block, twelve cells, twelve fritters. The Hole was always full. Most of the inmates were there for ten days and released, but I stayed.

The guard appeared at the front of my cell. The greasy fritter was handed through the narrow slit in the door. Anger forced me not to respond to the guard's "How you doin'?" I wanted to refuse the fritter, to show some sign of rebellion for the indignation I felt, but hunger and survival instincts were too strong and I kept silent. The fritter was warm. I separated the two slices of bread and deposited the greasy fritter in the corner of my cell for the now familiar aging process. It replaced the previous day's fritter, which was now ready to be consumed. This was an important ritual, the highlight of my day.

I took the dried fritter and ate it slowly. I ate one slice of bread and saved the second one for later.

When I'd finished my meal, I would crawl into the makeshift hammock and swing back and forth, trying to close my mind to reality. Often I lay there searching my soul for the reason of my existence. Sometimes I was fortunate enough to drift into a semi-conscious state of mind where hurt and pain disappeared. Gradually the boredom was replaced by a purple haze of tranquility.

The days wore on. Inmates were released or taken out to court, but I remained. When the shadows began to drift through the skylight, I knew it was time for the inmate crews to return to their cells in the world outside the Hole. I could hear the clanging of doors. Voices and laughter came through and I cursed the bastards who had me locked in this dungeon. They ought to start a riot and have me busted out of here! But no one did.

I heard the muffled announcement for "chow time" followed by banging doors and more laughter. The sounds sent pain and anguish through my body. Memories of hot coffee, the huge dining room and trays of hot food made the hunger seem unbearable. Just to be a part of the prison population seemed like the ultimate goal. The "streets" were no longer uppermost in my mind. Getting the hell out of the Hole was all I cared about.

When the day was over, inmates in the Hole began to fight back the night and the intense loneliness that it brought. "You want to play a game of twenty questions, Gordy?"

"Who's gonna play?"

"No fuckin' cheatin', Charley."

"Shit, man, you're the one who cheats." The game began and continued into the night until it ended in an argument or accusations of cheating and threats of bodily harm.

It was late and the outer cell blocks were quiet. "Let's flood this son-of-a-bitch!"

"Fuck you, man. I'm on the bottom tier."

"Start banging your doors. Let's wake those bastards up out there." The insanity had begun again.

Finally, it was quiet. I tried to fall asleep. I counted sheep and read the Bible, never really sure why I read it, except that it was there. Sleep came, somehow, and released my mind one more time.

Then came morning and the sounds of flushing toilets. The first grey streaks of daylight poked through the skylight and it started all over again.

"I'm gonna get out today."

"Where's those fuckin' fritters?"

"Dave cut his wrists last night. You hear them take him out?"

"They'll bring him back soon as they sew him up."

"What the fuck is this all about, God?" But there was no answer.

Then a year had passed, 365 calendar days, and I was released from the Hole.

The institution had changed. The warden, the associate warden, and the captain had been fired. A new administration had been brought in and sweeping changes had been made. The inmates' power to control jobs and favors had been eliminated. No more buying a good job. No special favors were allowed. No more paying rent to live in a better cell. Most of all, the value of belonging to a gang or a clique was almost non-existent. The inmate leadership was gone, leaving a tremendous void in the inmate power structure.

When I was released from isolation, I was looked upon with awe and disbelief. Those who knew me greeted me with admiration, as if I were a returning hero. The new inmates had heard of me. I was given a wide berth and silent respect, a respect that made my life easier in the years to come.

That first day out of the Hole, I walked into the mess hall for chow. My bluejeans were tied with a string to keep them from falling off my bony hips. My cheekbones were sunken, giving me a skeletal appearance. The inmates there shook my hand, slapped my back, and hollered my name in praise of my ordeal. In the days and months that followed, I found myself placed in the void of leadership that now existed. More and more the inmates looked to me for support and guidance.

The year in the Hole had changed me dramatically. The hours of isolation and loneliness had slowly brought me to the realization that if I ever wanted to get out of prison, I'd have to learn to play the Man's game. I had to be less of a tough guy and more of a diplomat, especially with the administration. I had to develop a positive role.

I began to get involved in some of the programs and activities that were looked upon with favor by the new administration. "You've got to show them what they want to see" was the common theme among the inmates in dealing with the new authorities.

I went to work in the kitchen preparing the vegetables and then gradually moved to the position of supervisor. I took it upon myself to personally prepare the fritters that were served to the convicts in the Hole. This gave me the opportunity to subtly strike back at the Man and assist the guys locked in the Hole. I would add a healthy portion of ground beef to the mixture of vegetables that made up the patties. It gave me great satisfaction to know that the guard was delivering semi-hamburgers to the inmates in the Hole instead of the fritters of old.

I started to "fit" in the society that made up the prison culture. I was adjusting to my environment. The violence of the riot was not forgotten. It still lingered in my mind, but it was pushed aside in the struggle for survival in the dog-eat-dog world of prison.

A change in me was gradually taking place, and the "naive kid" was becoming a sophisticated convict leader, a role that would control my life for years to come.

6. Transfer to Walla Walla

While it was still dark, the prison guards were finishing with the hand cuffs and chains, preparing us for the long ride from Monroe to Walla Walla.

Again I'd been in the Hole, this time for instigating a food strike. The administration had decided to transfer a number of us to Walla Walla, the state's maximum security prison. "We'll see how tough you bastards are when they get you at 'the Walls.' " The guards seemed to enjoy putting the fear of God into our hearts. Whatever their motives were, the fear they instilled had its effect.

A double wrap of chain around our waists was secured with a master padlock. Handcuffs were snapped tightly on our wrists and anchored to the waist chain. A heavy length of chain tied us together like link sausages, and to complete the package for shipping, leg irons were attached. With a smirk, the guard said, "Okay, let's go. Stay together boys." We shuffled awkwardly down a hallway to the barred metal "sally port" doors. We worked our way carefully down a long flight of stairs. Streaks of daylight were beginning to break the early morning darkness.

We were a grotesque, eerie sight. Flanked by prison guards, ten shackled inmates, chains rattling, cursed as we stumbled in step toward the waiting prison van. The van was dark green, the windows small and narrow with wire mesh covering each of them. Inside, benches jammed tightly together ran down each side. Each bench would hold up to five prisoners. The back of the van had a heavy wire gate secured by a large padlock and thick metal doors that closed the van off like a coffin. Heavy screens separated the driver and gun guard from the inmates. The guard rode with a riot gun resting on his lap as a constant reminder to the shackled prisoners. The van was infamous throughout the state prison system and was aptly named "The Green Hornet."

The guard was talking as the van slowly pulled away. "It's going to be a long ride. We'll be stopping once for gas. You can use the restroom then. If you can't hold it, you'll have to go through the screen in the back of the van. We've got sack lunches. I don't want any trouble. No smoking, no rocking the van, just sit back and we'll get you to your new home sometime this afternoon." He turned and said something to the driver and they both laughed.

The inmates were quiet. We'd all made our declarations about leaving that stinking Monroe behind us and getting to a joint where we'd be treated like men. I was shackled next to Bob, who'd become a partner of mine. He was doing time for burglary and didn't seem to fit the prison world. We'd been involved in athletics together. Both of us had been the joint champions in our respective weight divisions on the boxing team. Most of the ten inmates were being transferred because they were labelled troublemakers by the administration.

I'd been in Monroe twice and had developed a reputation as a "bad" dude. My parole, after the riot and my year in the Hole, had lasted only a couple of months. Frustrated and angry at my inability to make it on the outside, I struck out at the prison administration. It was this kind of rebellious attitude that led to my ride in the Green Hornet. I was on my way to the Walls.

Charlie, an older inmate, had requested that he go to the Walls because he'd been there before and didn't want to do time with the "kids" at Monroe. He was busy telling a couple of youngsters how to get along at the Walls. "Man, you just do your own time. Don't borrow cigarettes, and be careful who you accept anything from. The 'Jockers' are always trying to get some young 'pink' kid in debt. Then, when he can't pay, they make a joint punk out of him."

"Lefty," a tall lanky inmate who'd been complaining for miles about having to take a 'piss,' spoke up: "Man, if you don't stop this son-of-a-bitch, I'm going to piss all over the van."

The gun guard, sounding as though he was making a real sacrifice, said, "Okay, we're gonna pull off. Move to the back and we'll open the doors. You can go through the screen." The van slowed to a stop on the shoulder of the highway. Lefty was in the middle of the chain, but after much shoving and cursing, we managed to position him so he was facing the screen.

"Man, I can't go like this," he pleaded.

"It's that or you do it in your pants. We aren't opening these doors until we get to Yakima," the guard snapped.

"Man, go ahead. I can't stand like this very long," another inmate complained. Lefty unzipped his pants and relieved himself. I'd rather go in my pants than go through that hassle, I thought. Now other inmates were declaring their need to urinate. Each time an inmate had finished, we'd move the chain of bodies until another person was positioned at the gate at the back of the van.

"Hey, man, get your fingers out of my ass," someone yelled. Everyone laughed, and pushed harder against the screen. The inmate who was trying to get his pants zipped was trapped.

"Hey, man, knock it off. You're breaking my balls!"

The gun guard was trying to restore order. "Okay, back to your seats, you guys. Knock off the shit. We'll be in Yakima in less than an hour. The rest of you can wait till we get there."

He slammed the metal doors in the face of the inmate jammed against the screen. We scrambled for our seats, falling against each other as the driver slammed the Green Hornet into gear and pulled back onto the highway. Our next stop was the state garage in Yakima. It was the halfway point. The guards gassed up the van and handed out the sack lunches. It felt good to get out of the van and to stretch my legs.

"Okay, let's go!" The rest was over.

"There it is," Charlie said.

"I don't see anything," another prisoner snapped. The long ride had taken most of the day. Tempers were getting short. Everyone was crowding, trying to see through the narrow window of the van.

"See that smokestack on the hill?" Charlie pointed. "That's the joint. We're almost there."

I could see the tall red smokestack in the distance. "Man, I'm glad of that. My ass feels like one big blister," I said. My legs and back ached from the long ride and my clothes were soaked with perspiration. The last hundred miles had been unbearable. You could see the bleak, grey walls more clearly as we climbed the long sloping hill that led to the prison. It looks like a tough son-of-a-bitch, I thought.

A building shaped like a spoked wheel lay some distance from the Walls. "What's that building over there?" someone asked.

"That's the minimum security building. When you get near the end of your sentence, they let you move out there to work on the farm," Charlie answered.

"Man, it's a big bastard," someone commented.

"There's 1500 convicts in there," Charlie stated.

You could see the gun towers atop the high stone walls. Man, that's a prison, I thought. We'd pulled into a parking area at the front of the prison and the driver and gun guard got out. They were now talking to the guard who'd come out of the building to meet the van. "We got ten tough ones from Monroe for ya'." The driver was talking loud enough for us to hear.

"We'll take the toughness out of them. Let's get 'em out and get 'em processed." The guard's voice sounded threatening.

The sound of the key turning in the door lock was loud inside the confines of the van. No one had spoken for the past two or three miles. The gun guard pulled the door open. "Let's go. Everybody out."

When I stepped out of the van, the heat hit me like a blast from a furnace. The hot afternoon sun caused vapor-like heat waves to bounce off the soft black asphalt. I could see into the gun tower on top of the wall over our heads. The guard stood staring down at us. He had a rifle cradled in the crook of his arm. Dark sun glasses gave him an ominous look.

The guard led us up a short flight of stairs into the administration building. We stumbled along behind him, chains rattling, each of us trying to coordinate our steps with the inmate in front of us.

At the top of the stairs, a long hallway led to a huge barred cage. On one side of the cage, a guard stood behind a thick glass partition in what looked like a control booth. "We got ten transfers from Monroe." The guard handed a folder through a small slit in the glass booth. Another guard opened the gate that led into the barred cage. "Let's go." He stood back as we shuffled single file through the gate. When we were all inside, the guard slammed the gate shut and locked it with a huge key that he kept in a holster on his belt. The gun guard was still with us and he began to unlock the chains that hooked us together. He handed the other guard a handcuff key and the cuffs were removed. I rubbed my wrists. There were red welts where the cuffs had been. I shook my hands to speed up the return of circulation.

"Okay, listen up," ordered the guard who'd met the van. He had lieutenant bars on his shirt and spoke with authority. "We're going to take you outside. You'll be issued new clothes and given a hair cut. Then you'll take a shower and be sprayed with disinfectant. You'll be staying in the fish tank for thirty days. There will be two of you in each cell, so if you've got someone you want to cell with, you let the officer know." He barked the information like a drill sergeant.

"What about our property? When do we get that?" Charlie asked.

"You'll get it in a day or two. Let's go. You all stay together." The guard in the cage opened another metal door that led into another world.

7. Walls

Fear of the known and unknown blended together, causing knots in my stomach. Damp rivulets of perspiration ran down my sides under the loose-fitting denim shirt. The stark realities of prison engulfed me and I felt like screaming, "Stop, damn it, I don't want to go through those fucking doors!" All the pain, anguish and violence of my first experiences at Monroe flashed through my mind. I turned to Bob, our eyes met, and I could sense his fear. "Let's go, man. Looks like this'll be home for a while." We followed the guard through the doorway. I had learned to survive in Monroe, but Walla Walla had its own set of rules. Survival in the Walls was another story.

From inside, the institution looked gigantic. Large red cell blocks surrounded by tall grey walls were scattered across acres of land. Heat waves danced off them as we followed the lieutenant along a sidewalk that led through the prison grounds. Inmates lounging in the shade eyed us as we walked along. Mean lookin' bastards, I thought.

As we made our way through the grounds, inmates who knew Charlie were greeting him: "Couldn't stay away? What'd you get busted for, man? You're gonna be my old lady this time." The voices jeered.

"This is a big son-of-a-bitch, man." I looked at Bob.

"Yeah, man, this place gives me the creeps." His voice was low.

We entered a long narrow cell block. "This is one-wing. You'll be living here for your first thirty days," the lieutenant said. The inside of the building was hot. It was all metal and the August sun beat down without mercy, turning the cell block into a sweltering inferno.

A guard met us at the front of a huge complex referred to as a "wing" in Walla Walla. "Go over to those benches and strip down." He pointed to a row of wooden benches. There were ten neatly stacked bundles that looked like our new clothes. "After you've stripped, go into the shower and get sprayed."

I took off the sweaty blue denim shirt and sat down, untied my shoes and pulled them off. I took my pants off and kicked them into the growing pile of dirty clothes in the center of the room. Son-of-a-bitch, I hate this shit! I kicked the brown shorts across the floor and walked naked into the shower room. An inmate stood just inside the door with a metal spray gun. The odor of disinfectant filled the room.

"Okay, raise your arms." The inmate moved toward me, the spray gun in his hands. I raised my arms and he pumped the gun, covering my body with the thin sticky liquid. It felt greasy and brought tears to my eyes.

"Son-of-a-bitch, keep that shit out of my eyes!" I moved away from him.

"Hey, man, I'm just doin' my job. Ain't no use gettin' hot at me." He was an older guy and seemed sincere.

"Okay, but watch where you're pointing that fucking thing."

"You gotta turn around and bend over." He sounded apologetic. I could feel the heat of embarrassment run through me. I bent over. "Spread your cheeks. Okay, hit the showers." I walked across the room to the line of showers. Some of my traveling companions were already under the water, washing off the sticky spray. I turned my shower on and picked up a large brown bar of soap from the shower floor. When I'd washed away the disinfectant, I turned the shower on cold. The cool water soothed me. I turned it cooler and cooler until I shivered from the cold. "Let's go. Out of the shower," barked the lieutenant.

The convict who'd manned the spray gun threw me a towel. "Get yourself dried and dressed and then get in line for a hair cut. Two barber chairs sat at the end of the cell block. The barbers were convicts and the hair cuts took about two minutes each. Clippers went up one side and down the other until my head was bare and only a prickly stubble was left. The barbers seemed to enjoy their work and joked with each other as they butchered us. Bastards, I hope I get the chance to pay you back. I was angry!

"When you're done, report to the wing sergeant for your cell assignment," ordered the lieutenant. Bob and I walked to the desk at the front of the wing. We'd decided to cell together. A guard with a sergeant's insignia on his shirt sat behind a desk. Beads of sweat covered his forehead. His grey shirt was damp with perspiration. The fan behind him was doing little good.

"We want a cell together, if we can. I'm Graham and this is Schwarder." The sergeant ran his fingers down a board with names beside each number.

"Okay, you guys will be in 6-C. That's the third tier on the left side of the wing. Pick up blankets and sheets and I'll let you in your cell." The cell block was four tiers high. The cell Bob and I were assigned, on the third tier, was even hotter than the bottom floor.

The cells were smaller than the cells in Monroe, and two men shared each small cubicle. The metal bunks, one on top of the other, hung by chains from the wall. The toilet was a bucket filled with lime water, and a small metal pan served as a sink for shaving or washing yourself.

Our short-cropped hair and loose-fitting blue denims made us look like the leading characters in an old prison movie. Suddenly, we both started laughing. "Man, you look like a convict. You got enough scars on your head to hold six weeks of rain." Bob's head was bare and the old scars stood out like beacons.

"You ain't no prize, man. Them pants are big enough for two people," Bob laughed.

Bob had a good sense of humor. He was a good athlete and a tough guy. We'd become friends in Monroe and got along most of the time.

The one issue during our stay in the "fish tank" that caused us to get angry with each other was the daily trip to the "honey dew line." This name was "affectionately" given to the daily ritual of emptying the bucket, the make-shift toilet provided in each cell. The ritual was degrading and was one that we continually argued over. We tried to solve the conflict by playing cards, loser drawing the dreaded chore, but the games usually ended in accusations of cheating and one or the other refusing to pay. Each day for thirty days we would vow never to make the trip to the "shit trough" again, but each day one of us would take the bucket and grudgingly fall into the "honey dew line."

There was always a group of "old timers" who greeted you with jeers and laughter as you made your way down the courtyard. "What you carrying there, Gordy?"

"The sweet smell of success."

"How you like the 'honey dew line,' fish?" another voice chimed in.

The 100 degree heat made it essential that the bucket be emptied, or the smell would become unbearable in the hot cell. Each day seemed to bring us a little closer to a violent outbreak over the never ending issue of the "honey dew line." Somehow we survived and each day one of us would make the long walk with the bucket of waste, holding his breath as he emptied the bile into the huge trough at the end of the courtyard.

Walla Walla was huge compared to Monroe. There were seven monstrous cell blocks, two large dining rooms that were separated by the inmate kitchen, a red brick school building, and a powerhouse with a smokestack that reached high into the air. The institution had the appearance of a small industrial community. However, the twenty-two-foot cement walls with manned gun towers, where guards kept a twenty-four hour vigil over the fifteen hundred inmates housed within, were a constant reminder that you were in a maximum security prison.

I wasn't the same naive kid who'd entered Monroe six years earlier. I'd become a fighter, both in and out of the ring, but fear was always with me. I had learned to disguise it behind anger and aggressiveness. I'd matured into a survivor in the prison world. My reputation had preceded me, and the various cliques and inmate groups tried to recruit Bob and me, hoping we'd join their ranks. Candy, cigarettes and offers to move into certain cells were delivered to us from inmate leaders.

Bob and I were not "joiners," but had become "adjusters," reconciled to the abnormal culture that was prison life. We both disliked the bullies and gangs that exist in the prison society and wanted no part of them. So we'd return the gifts and turn down the offers to become members of the respective gangs. The inmates who had transferred to the Walls with me looked to me for strength and support. Occasionally, a book, some candy or a note would be delivered from someone we'd known in Monroe. These offerings had quite a different meaning. Six years ago, the offers would have been offensive and accepting them could have meant you might be expected to give sexual favors to the donor. Now, they meant we "had arrived" in the prison culture.

Fear and violence are a constant part of prison life and can destroy and humiliate those who are not physically or mentally strong. These conditons, so prevalent in Walla Walla, brought a new reality into my world. I looked at the old men who walked the yard, heads down, their lives over. They had a sobering effect on me. These men had grown old in prison and would die in this cold, wearing world.

Bob interrupted my thoughts as we were walking across the prison yard. "Poor sons-a-bitches. Prison sure ain't no place for an old man." Bob and I looked around the yard at the old men, some of whom had been in prison for fifteen and twenty years. They had stopped wanting out and had become a part of this world of cell blocks, yard-outs and isolation. "I sure as hell don't want to grow old in this son-of-a-bitch!" I said.

"Yeah, man, I just want to do my time and get out of here."

We were on our way back from classification. Our thirty days were up and we were about to move out into the main population. We'd both been assigned to work in the kitchen and wanted to keep our noses clean and do our "own time."

8. "Bruno" as an Escape

I watched Bob as we walked along. He was a good person and I couldn't understand how he'd wound up in prison. Hell, he had a family, had been an all-state football player and had a lot of good things going for him. He was doing time for assault after a drinking spree. It seemed all his trouble stemmed from booze. Bob turned around and spoke. "Yeah, I think celling together is a good idea. We don't have to empty any more shit buckets, so we should get along okay."

"I think you owe me two days anyway," I laughed.

The lieutenant in the control room in charge of assigning cells was a grey-haired man who had the mannerisms of a fussy old grandmother. He explained all the reasons why it would be difficult to assign Bob and me to the same cell. When he finally agreed to the request, it was with a deep sigh of indignation, as though we were taking advantage of his good nature. I couldn't tell if he was serious or if his mannerisms were just a habit.

We picked up our belongings and walked across the dusty compound to seven-wing. There was a desk at the front of the cell block. The guard sitting behind the desk looked up as Bob and I walked in. "We're supposed to move into 8-A." When I spoke, an inmate leaning against the desk looked up.

"Does Willie know you guys are moving in?" He looked at the

guard with what appeared to be an expression of disgust.

"I don't think so, but the lieutenant in the control room told us to move in there."

"What's your names?" The guard stood up; he had a clipboard in his hands. We told him our names and he turned to the inmate. "Type name cards and put them on the kitchen roster, and show them where they'll cell. Then you two go over to the clothing room and check out some whites and pick up blankets. Do ya' know where the clothing room is located?" He sounded like a pretty good guy.

"No, we just got out of the fish tank and don't know much about anything yet," Bob answered. He sounded angry and I nudged him with my elbow. I sure as hell didn't want to start no shit. Bob had a temper and could create a shit storm in a minute.

"You go down the walk toward the mess hall. It's the last door in this building. Just tell them you're goin' to work in the kitchen and you need whites and blankets." The guard's voice didn't change and I felt relieved.

The cell block had the familiar smell of disinfectant, but the cells were larger than any I'd seen before. Two double bunks, one on each side of the cell, took up a large part of the interior. The familiar toilet and sink were bolted to the center of the back wall, but there were also pictures on the walls and a table with a straight-backed chair between the two bunks. Compared to the steel cubicles where we'd spent the past thirty days, the cell looked almost luxurious.

When we had located our cell, the guard opened the door to the cell block and we walked back out into the bright afternoon sun. "Did you get the feeling that they ain't too excited about us moving in?" Bob was hot.

"Yeah, man, but let's not start any shit," I cautioned.

The dusty courtyard was hot and muggy as we walked along the sidewalk that ran the length of seven-wing. We walked through a barred metal door that led into the clothing room. Two inmates and a huge, overweight prison guard were sorting through baskets of blue denim clothing. We stopped at a large counter that separated us from long rows of shelves that were stacked with assorted clothing, sheets and blankets. The mattresses were piled to the ceiling against one wall. They were thick and looked new. I thought of the paper-thin mattresses that we'd had in the fish tank.

"What do you two want?" The guard's voice was threatening.

"They sent us over to get some whites and blankets. We just got out of the fish tank." I tried to sound friendly and innocent.

"Where the hell you been? You're supposed to come here first. The rest of the fish have already got their shit." The guard had walked over to the counter and was leaning over. His close-cropped, grey hair was damp with sweat and you could smell the musty odor of his body as he glared at us.

"We checked into seven-wing first. We thought that's what we were supposed to do." I could feel the anger swell in my gut. The fat son-of-a-bitch, how the hell were we supposed to know!

"Well, let's get them fixed up." He turned to one of the inmates working on the bin of clothes.

"You guys goin' to work in the kitchen?" the inmate asked in a friendly voice.

"Yeah, they told us to get sheets, blankets and white clothes," Bob answered.

"What size pants you wear?" He had a pencil and a yellow pad of paper on the counter in front of him. "I'll need your names and your joint numbers." He scribbled our names and we told him our pant size. "How about shirts? You want long sleeves or short?" We both said short sleeves. The temperature was still in the high nineties. Shit, what kind of question was that?

The other inmates had joined us and began asking questions.

"Where you guys from?"

"How much time you doin'?"

"Where you celling?"

"They put us in 8-A in seven-wing. Do you know the guys living there?" I asked.

"Yeah, that's Willie's cell. He's an okay dude." We picked up the clothes and blankets and with our arms loaded, we walked back to seven-wing.

There were two other inmates in the cell when we arrived. They had the lower bunks occupied. I spread my blankets on one of the top bunks and Bob took the other. "I'm Gordy Graham and this is Bob Schwarder. I guess we'll be your new cell partners for a while."

The two inmates, both dressed in white pants and shirts, grunted. "I'm Willie and this is Leroy, Roy for short. Where'd they put you guys to work?" He sounded friendly enough.

"We're supposed to work in the dish tank, whatever that is."

"Yeah, they always put the fish in that sweat box."

Leroy was talking. "You keep your nose clean, you won't be there over a week or two. We're both in the bakery. It's a good go. You can get better chow and stay drunk half the time if you play it cool. You guys drink? You're looking at the best moonshiner in the joint! You guys want a drink?" Leroy sounded like he had already had one too many.

Willie looked angrily at him. "Son-of-a-bitch, you're gonna get us busted. You want everybody to know your business."

"Hey, man, what you do is your business," I said. Before I could say any more, Bob had already answered.

"Sure, man, what you got?"

"We got some 'raisin jack.' It's been down three days and it's good." Leroy seemed unaware of Willie's anger.

Leroy walked over to a stool sitting at the back of the cell. He lifted the lid off and pulled out a plastic gallon jug. "One of you watch for the Man. There's a mirror in the bars." Leroy was pouring four cups full of the yellowish liquid. The fermented smell seemed strong. I peered up and down the catwalk in front of the cells, holding the small broken mirror through the bars. I could see to both ends of the tier. There was no one in sight, and I took one of the cups from Leroy and gulped down a big swallow of "raisin jack." The sharp sting of alcohol brought tears to my eyes and I began to cough noisily.

"Shit, man, this stuff is powerful!"

"It's three cup shit. You'll be walking backwards if you take more than three."

"Hell, I think two cups will knock me on my ass. I haven't had a drink in months. They never made much booze in Monroe. Once in a while when I was working in the kitchen, we'd make some, but we never had anything this strong. How do you make it?"

"You need a cup or two of raisins, a small piece of yeast and three cups of sugar. Let it stand for three days in a warm place. Add sugar a couple of times if you want it really potent. It smells like hell, so you need a rubber hose too. Put one end of the hose in the jug and run the other end into a pan of water—that kills the smell. They got a screw in the kitchen who has a nose like a bloodhound. They call him 'bug eyes.' Man, he's always sniffing for 'pruno.' You'll meet him. But we keep two or three batches going all the time, so if he busts one, we got another one started." Bob had already finished his cup and was pouring another.

I had just emptied my second cup. My head was getting light, and I could feel the alcohol tingle in my belly. "Want another one?" Roy had the jug out again. His face was getting flushed and his hand was shaky as he held the half-full jug out to me.

"Sure, what the hell. This stuff is good. I can feel it already."

Bob was on his fourth cup. "I appreciate you guys turning us on."

"That's okay, man. We score regular and cell partners are in. We get some speed once in a while too. You take any speed?"

"I used to drop some valo in Monroe, but I ain't into drugs. I'm a fighter. I was the middleweight champion in Monroe. What kind of fighters they got here?"

"They got some tough bastards. There's a middleweight named Tex. He's the champ. There's a card coming up on Labor Day. You ought to get on it." Willie sounded excited and half drunk.

"Who do we see about a fight?" I asked. "My partner's a light heavy and he's tough, punches like hell. We're both gonna fight."

"They got a black dude who can really box. He's the light heavy but he ain't got no heart. I'll talk to the guy who's making the matches and see if he can get you on the card. If you guys challenge for the joint championships, they'll put you on the card for sure. They ain't got nobody to fight Tex."

"Man, I'm going over to the kitchen and get something to eat." Leroy was putting on his shoes.

"You better stay in the cell, man. You'll get busted. You smell like a brewery," Willie said.

"Fuck 'em, man, I ain't gonna get busted!" Leroy looked shaky as he moved to the front of the cell and began to holler, "Key up 8-A!" He yelled again, "Key up 8-A!"

"Hold it down, man. I'm on nights." The voice came from somewhere above us in the cell block.

"Fuck you and your night shift!" Leroy's voice had turned to a snarl.

"Hey, man, cool it. That's Whitey," Willie pleaded. "Man, you don't need no heat. You just got out of the Hole and they'll bury you if you get busted again."

"Fuck 'em." Leroy was quieter now. He wasn't drunk enough to ignore Willie's warning. I could hear the lock box open and a click as the cell door was released. Leroy pulled it open and stepped out onto the tier.

"Man, I better go with him. Shit, he's liable to get busted." Willie was putting on his shirt as he hurried after him.

"Man, this ain't bad. These guys are okay." I climbed up on my bunk. The "raisin jack" had made me lightheaded and I felt good.

"The Walls ain't too bad. Sure as hell beats Monroe." Bob's voice sounded fuzzy as I dozed off to sleep.

9. The Art of Manipulation

My experience at Monroe had taught me that fighting the system was a losing proposition. When I had gotten settled into the routine of Walla Walla, I began to explore the ways to get myself out. There was escape, an alternative always being considered. There were elaborate schemes for escape continually being planned. Most of the escapes never took place, and those that did were generally unsuccessful. There was usually a tunnel being dug somewhere in the joint. Plans for going over the wall by rope or ladder or a scheme to walk out the front gate disguised as a visitor or a guard were always a part of inmate conversation. The dream of escape kept some inmates alive. It gave them a reason to get up in the morning. Beneath the dream of escape lay the reality of the parole board.

One old con put it this way: "You can't just lay back and do your time. If you do, the parole board will make you do it all. The parole board is all-powerful. Parole board members can let you out in six months or in five years. You've got to get into something that will make them think you're rehabilitated."

I knew from experience in Monroe that the parole board was indeed all-powerful. The members met each month and evaluated the progress of the inmates who appeared before them. If you were involved in education or vocational training, your chances of favorable action by the board increased. The sentence had no bearing on the parole board's action. If your initial court sentence was five years, you could do anywhere from one year to the full five. It was left to the discretion of the board.

Rumors were always rampant in the joint as to just what you needed to do to increase your chances of favorable action from the board. One opinion was that if you messed up when you first arrived and then straightened out, it was an indication that you were rehabilitated. The parole board members would then give you an early release. Another popular rumor held that the only way to get out was to get an education or learn a vocational trade. The board looked at this as a clear indication that you were serious about staying out of prison. There were also rumors that certain board members could be paid off. It was said that if you had the right connections on the "streets," the board's decision could be swayed in your favor. I was willing to try any and all of these if it meant an early release.

Some inmate was always bragging about his connections outside, an uncle who had political clout or a partner who'd offer the board big money to shorten a prison term. This kind of influence, whether real or imaginary, made the convict feel like somebody people cared about. It gave him a sense of importance. The loneliness and frustration of prisons create this incredible, constant need for recognition as a person, not just another number. But while I, like the others, schemed to get out, I had to survive within.

There was a distinct difference in the attitudes and life styles of the inmates at Walla Walla. It was a much more serious population. Men who were doing life sentences and those who had been in prison most of their adult lives gave the institution a more stable atmosphere. New inmates who caused unnecessary problems could expect to be visited by one or more of the "old cons" and to have the ways of life "gently" explained to them.

Yet the leaders were dangerous; some were known killers. People doing life in prison have less tolerance for the stool pigeons and the braggarts. In Monroe, disagreements would be settled with fists. In Walla Walla, they used knives.

The prison atmosphere was tempered by the awareness of this solemn undercurrent, and the population adjusted accordingly. It is an abnormal existence where right and wrong depend on the person committing the act. It is an environment where dishonesty, fear and compromise become a way of life. It is an environment where you live, eat and sleep with known murderers, where you are reminded constantly that life is cheap and that there is little concern about what happens to men and women in prisons.

The fact that someone has been stabbed for not paying a carton of cigarettes owed to a loan shark doesn't cause a ripple of concern. Witnessing an inmate being brutally beaten because he has talked to someone's "queen" or is suspected of being an informer reinforces the fear and gradually molds the behavior of the prison population.

The negative prison environment gradually begins to distort reality. The person who enters prison for committing a bad act becomes a bad person. Wrong is rationalized as right if the act is against the Man or the system. At first, the inmate rejects this abnormal value structure, but gradually he finds himself caught up in it.

The "convict code" is accepted and becomes stronger than the rules established by the Man. Many convicts, young and old, will choose to serve time in the Hole and give up their release dates rather than violate it. The do's and don't's that make up the "convict code" are clear, and violators are subject to instant retaliation by their peers. You don't snitch to the Man, you don't steal from your brother, you don't talk to the Man except on business, you don't prey on the "good convicts," you support opposition to the Man even if it's insane, you don't talk to snitches or child molesters, you don't offend or mistreat women visitors. These were all silent, unwritten rules that convicts knew and understood.

If you didn't have a strong personal foundation or loved ones, you could satisfy your need for belonging within the prison culture. The more you rebelled against the Man, the more you were accepted in prison. You became the "good convict," a man of stature. If a movie had been made to depict the image of a "good convict," my life could have served as the example. There were things I would do at the expense of my freedom. There were things I would oppose to the ultimate, even though this might cause me to suffer or go to the Hole. The expectations of others and the desire to be a part of something were strong. But what makes you "belong" inside the prison, makes it hard for you to succeed "outside."

The ability to adjust upon release becomes increasingly difficult once you establish a strong personal identity in prison. The same qualities that made you a "good convict" are liabilities on "the street." You lose your identity, and you don't fit outside. To kill the disharmony, you seek out other ex-convicts. You know that to interact with these people is a violation of the parole rules, but the need to be with someone who thinks as you do is very strong.

On the outside, decisions are made the same way they are in prison: values are based on "the code." Your friends expect you to exhibit the same behavior outside as you did in prison. Because you need to belong, you fulfill their expectations. Deep down you know that it is wrong and that you will wind up back in prison, but you do it anyway. You camouflage this awareness by living a frantic life style, blocking the reality that you are living on borrowed time. Every day and night is full of action. You live as though there's no tomorrow because you know that tomorrow you may find yourself back behind bars.

No one openly speaks of getting busted or going back to prison, but everyone knows. It's always "just one more caper and I'm getting myself straightened out." It's an unrealistic world that leads to "doing life" on the "installment plan." The fear of dying at the wrong end of a gun or from an overdose of drugs is everpresent.

The longer this lifestyle continues, the more difficult it is to break the cycle. The time on "the streets" gets shorter and the prison sentences increase. Two years, to five, then ten, and on to life in the Walls. And you find yourself caught in the investment trap. "Man, I've done so much time, someone's got to pay before I quit." You're always trying to catch up, to make society pay for all the time you've done in prison—and you end up doing more.

Words that once sounded exciting and real become hollow and

meaningless. "When I get out, man, I'm going to make one big hit and get myself a little businesss and square up. You won't see me back, man. I'm going to get me a job and an old lady and carry a lunch pail." Statements like these have echoed down every corridor and bounced off every steel bar in every prison in this country. These proclamations are made with deep conviction, but they are made in a controlled environment, an environment where basic human needs are met and the accountability for decisions has been forfeited. In the "real world," commitments made in prison get lost in the struggle for survival.

This kind of environment slowly changed me from a young, scared kid who fought for survival and actively opposed brutality, to a tough, manipulative convict. I began rationalizing wrong. I bought into the "convict code" 100%. In my mind, at that time, it was right.

The Man did not control the community inside the Walls; it was controlled by the convict leadership. You bought your space with fists, knives or cigarettes, or you survived at the expense of your manhood by tip-toeing through prison as a conformist. A violation of the "conivict code" could mean getting beaten by other cons, being locked in protective custody, or being ostracized. It could even mean death. This abnormal existence scars the soul of each and every person who lives through the experience.

To function effectively in this environment, you need to accept some realities. You blind yourself to injustice. You don't compete for anything that puts you in conflict with the gangs or cliques. You don't show love or warmth, don't borrow or gamble, don't get involved in drugs, and don't fraternize with the Man. If you learn these rules, you can survive. If you don't, life can be a series of hellish days and fearful nights.

The Walls was in a constant state of unrest during those first years of incarceration. The unrest had deep underlying causes, but the surface "causes" and results could be either serious or ludicrous. Hunger strikes were common and became an institutional joke. The strikes would start after breakfast and end before the evening meal. If there were a good movie scheduled, there would be no demonstration. The inmates who were the instigators generally made sure they'd filled their lockers from the inmate commissary before an impending strike. You could generally predict a hunger strike by observing certain inmate leaders' purchases.

Protests arose from concerns about food, visiting privileges, work, parole boards, guards' behavior or sometimes from just plain boredom. You could find support for almost any grievance in the prison environment. To test this theory, one of my partners began to solicit support for a strike protesting the lack of cartoons at the weekly movies. He soon had a following of inmates who supported the idea and a pamphlet was distributed throughout the institution asking inmates to stop eating until cartoons were added to the weekly movies. Had the issue been aggressively pursued, over one thousand adult males would have been starving themselves over Donald Duck and Mickey Mouse. The desire to strike back locks out logic and the insanity of the act becomes accepted behavior because of this.

Despite the insanity, inmates seem to naturally find their "places" in the prison culture. The hustlers find a way to hustle, gamblers find the poker games and the bookies, the dopers find the dope and the alcoholics find or make the alcohol. The workers find jobs and those seeking knowledge get into education. These categories make up a significant portion of the population within the Walls. But there is another group of inmates who seek power. These are the predators, the rip-off artists who seem to thrive on the prison environment.

A number of inmates become politically active. Prisons are fertile recruiting grounds for any revolutionary group. The idleness, anger and feeling of hopelessness cause inmates to strike out against the Man or the establishment. The prison administration and the guards represent the establishment, so any protest against the institution will find support. Men who have never voted or had any political affiliation become joint politicians.

Still others accept their fate and adjust comfortably to the prison world. Bridge, pinocle, poker, chess and checkers are played socially and as a way to gamble. Movies once a week, television, radio and social clubs become important activities. Prison jobs and educational or vocational training programs fill the hours for many inmates, nourished by their hopes for an early release. Hobbies, including leather craft, wood carving, painting and knitting, earn profits and fill the minds of those involved.

Then there were those inmates who didn't fit any of the normal patterns. They made up a small segment of the population that created constant management problems. They squirmed and fought against the restrictions like rainbow trout hooked in fast water. The prison became their platform for self justification. They realized the difference between right and wrong, but somehow were able to rationalize their own behavior, even though it might have been in direct violation of the prison rules. They established a very strong identity within the prison environment and received a great deal of feedback labeling them as "somebodies."

Somewhere in this complex world of thieves, murderers, misfits and malcontents, I developed an identity. I was always working toward release, but never able to see myself as anything other than a "good convict."

When I arrived, Walla Walla had few opportunities in educational or vocational training. There was a factory where inmates manufactured the car license plates for the state and a cannery that canned fruits and vegetables for Walla Walla and the other state institutions. The plate mill and cannery both offered jobs that paid an hourly wage to the inmate employee. The salaries started at four cents an hour and topped out at sixteen cents an hour. For many inmates, the salaries represented the only money they would see during their stay in the institution. To be making sixteen cents an hour was a significant accomplishment, and inmates who held these positions had a certain prestige.

The few vocational trades had long waiting lists of inmate applicants. There were a body and fender repair shop, a barber school, a small engine repair shop, and an office machine repair shop. The total number of inmates involved in vocational training programs at one time was around fifty. This situation created manipulation and caused unhealthy competition among the fifteen-hundred inmates.

A spot in a vocational trade almost assured you of a shortened prison term. It placed the prison officials who assigned inmates to these coveted positions in a power role. Each prison official would have an inmate clerk assigned to assist in clerical work and in screening applicants for the limited number of vacancies. The inmates in these jobs were generally the older, more sophisticated residents. They would gradually take over more of the responsibilities. If the staff person were lazy or didn't monitor activities closely, the inmate would become the deciding factor in the placement proceedings. This power put the inmate clerks in a position to manipulate the system and move their friends into these jobs.

There were certain inmate clerks who would exchange their support for a carton or two of cigarettes. This payment would assure you the privilege of being moved ahead of the less fortunate or less manipulative applicants. Inmates also acted as school teachers. Cigarettes would buy you high school credits. These practices were common knowledge and accepted procedure, though no one would openly admit that they were occurring.

I'd made up my mind not to recreate my old experiences at Monroe. I wanted out of this jungle! I began assessing all the information I'd been receiving on how to work the system. I started to look around for the easiest way to make my release happen. It seemed like the quickest way out was to get into a vocational program. It had to be something I could do on the "streets" to make an "honest living," a trade that the board would look upon favorably.

Bob and I had been working in the kitchen for about a month when Willie said he had a friend who could get us into barber school. "It's a good go, man, and the parole board gives good action to guys who complete barber school. My partner can set it up so you get a diploma and you won't have to go through all the shit." His voice took on a confidential tone even though we were the only ones in the cell. "It'll only cost you five cartons of cigarettes."

"I don't know, man. Putting your hands on someone else's funky head doesn't have much appeal. If there's a civilian instructor, how can your friend keep us from having to take the tests?" I knew that to be a barber, you had to take some kind of a test.

"Trust me, man. He's got it set up so he can switch the written tests and he's got the civilian wrapped up. All you have to do is put in the time and cut a head of hair once in a while."

"Let me think about it. I gotta do something. This kitchen is a drag. I've never seen so many dirty trays, and it sure as hell isn't something the parole board will cut your time over."

10. Playing the Game

My first attempt at release was the barber school. Willie's friend was able to manipulate the system and gain me early entry in spite of the long waiting list of inmates. It took me a very short time to discover that being a barber was not for me. I couldn't stand putting my hands on people's mangy heads. Learning the names of all the facial muscles and skin diseases wasn't much to my liking either. However, barber school did offer some fringe benefits that were appealing enough to cause me to stay and graduate. Frequent intoxication was one of them.

We had a civilian instructor who transferred the chore of ordering supplies to an inmate clerk. Each month the clerk would order an abundant supply of Budah, an aftershave lotion that was somewhere around 80 proof. It was no martini and a bitch to get down, but it was effective. Two good belts eliminated all worry, and being a barber, or a janitor, for that matter, became irrelevant. My barbering ability was questionable when I was sober; after a few belts of Budah, it was a disaster!

I became famous for my "Jack Dempsey" haircuts, and those inmates courageous enough to let me practice my work with a straight razor, often left my chair bleeding. I did graduate, thanks to my inmate friend's connection, and received a significant time cut from the board. I was released from the penitentiary and was back on the streets.

As in previous releases, I sought out my old friends, the only people I knew. Thieves, hustlers, and ex-cons made up my world. They were the only people I could communicate with. We understood each other. However, involvement with them was a sure ticket back to the joint. Six months later I was busted for burglary and returned to the institution to start anew. Fortunately for the inmate population, barber school was no longer an option.

This time around I chose the fight game. Surely I would get out and stay out on this "ticket." Boxing had always been a part of my life. I had developed good skills over the years. When I returned to prison, I worked to improve my boxing skills. I beat everyone in my weight class, then began to take on fighters in the heavier divisions.

I became the middleweight, light heavyweight, and heavyweight champion of the joint. I did have one strong competitor in the heavyweight division. I could beat him, but not consistently. But he was always in trouble and spent a great deal of his time in the Hole. When he was around, I would relinquish the heavyweight title to him. Otherwise, I held that title along with the others. I felt like I'd finally found something I was good at.

It was my intent to attract the attention of fight promoters and managers on the outside. When I began to get offers from the "streets," I was able to convince the parole board that I had found my niche in life. Again I was granted parole. I won a number of professional fights, but all the while, I was involved in safecracking and other dishonest activities. It wasn't long before I was back in Walla Walla, looking for a new way to beat the system.

The third time around I was able to manipulate the standard entry procedures and was accepted in the office machine repair school. Fortunately, I had a couple of partners who enrolled with me. Somehow, we were able to hang on by "the skin of our teeth" and we graduated.

The intricate movements of typewriter keys, platens and fulcrums haunted my dreams. But I survived and was released again to practice my trade. This time I secured a tool kit and applied for a job. I was hired as a typewriter repairman. My first and last morning on the job was an experience. I reported with my tool kit and the feeling that this was it, a job! Shit, I ain't never had one of these before!

The shop where I had applied for work was small. The work bench had been scarred by typewriters, calculators and screwdrivers. That morning the owner carried in my first repair job. I looked at it in dismay. It looked like a typewriter, but I had never seen one that had any similarities to the one being placed in front of me.

"This machine is skipping and the platen needs ground." The boss sounded bored.

"What kind is it?" I asked with embarrassment.

He gave me a look of disgust. "An I.B.M. Selectric. You have any experience on this type of machine?"

I felt cheated. Eighteen months of training and I hadn't even seen a machine like this. "Not really, but I can try." I didn't look up.

"I need someone experienced on I.B.M.s. Fifty percent of our work is on the Selectric." He walked away shaking his head. I knew he was thinking, "Those damned ex-cons." The frustration I felt consumed me. Where the hell do I fit, anyway? I didn't have any idea how to repair the complicated monster in front of me.

It wasn't long before I was back into my old habits. A short time later it was a ride in the Green Hornet and a "welcome home, Gordy." This time the vocational trades were exhausted, the fight game an unrealistic goal.

The only thing left was escape. The thought of escape absorbed me. I'd received a twelve year sentence for parole violation and burglary. I knew that I couldn't do that much time. I had to get out.

11. Escape for Real

In the past, I'd been involved in digging tunnels to escape. I instantly discovered that digging like a mole was not my style. I couldn't see myself making a suicide charge of the prison wall, and I was too well known to try to disguise myself as a guard or a visitor.

But I knew there had to be a way out.

The monotonous routine of prison life gradually molds prisoners and guards alike into patterns that become habitual. The longer the prisoner and guard are in the joint, the more predictable their behavior becomes. Inmates begin to adjust to the different attitudes and expectations of the correctional staff that monitors the activities within the prison. Some guards are alert and conscientious about their jobs and responsibilities while others are just trading time for a pay check and become unaware and irresponsible. Inmates adjust to both types. If they are going to do something that is against the regulations, they plan around the guards who are working a particular shift.

Walla Walla, like all of the older prisons in our country, was built to fill the needs of the time. As the needs increased, more cell blocks were added. When society began to shift from the concept of punishment for the sake of punishment to the concept of confinement for rehabilitation, the educational facilities and vocational shops were added. Industrial plants were constructed to keep the inmate busy. License plate mills, canneries, and furniture shops were built and offered productive use of inmate labor.

In Walla Walla, the cell blocks, educational facilities, kitchen, and dining areas were within a compound surrounded by high grey walls. The industrial area and the vocational shops were located in a large compound that butted up against one of the walls and was surrounded by a fence.

When entering the industrial area from the main compound, the inmates had to pass through a gate that was controlled by a guard in a gun tower atop the twenty-two-foot wall directly above the opening. At the foot of the wall, a guard monitored the flow of inmate traffic in and out of the area. A small shack was situated there to protect the guard from the heat of the summer and the cold of the Walla Walla winters.

Each inmate working in the industrial area was classified and photographed. This picture was then posted on a huge board in the guard's shack. As the inmates entered or left the area, the guard on duty would count the inmates and check them against the pictures on the board.

Ideally, this would serve as an effective control system.

In the evening, after the industrial area was cleared of inmates, one of the gun towers was left unmanned. When this occurred, it left a portion of the fenced area of the compound unprotected. If an inmate were left in the area after count had cleared, there would be an excellent chance to escape. He could scale the two cyclone fences topped with barbed wire, jump to the ground and be outside the prison where there was nothing but wheat fields between him and freedom.

That was the plan I had for escaping

I had observed that on rainy days the guard in the shack seldom came out to search inmates entering the industrial area. Materials and waste products were taken from the inside of the institution into the industrial area by wheelbarrow or cart. The wheelbarrow would be inspected by the security guard. But if the weather was bad, the guard would generally give it a cursory check from inside the warm, dry shack and wave it through into the industrial area.

I decided that the way to escape was to get into the industrial area without the guard seeing me by hiding in a wheelbarrow and waiting until everyone had been checked back into the main compound. With the guard tower unoccupied, I'd scale the fence and make my way to freedom.

They had been tearing down one of the old cell blocks and hauling the waste materials out into the industrial area. The waste would then be burnt or loaded onto trucks that would transport the waste to a nearby dump. One of my partners was working on the detail that was tearing down the cell block. I approached him with the idea of hiding me in one of the wheelbarrows and covering me with waste materials and boards. Then he could wheel me into the industrial area and I could escape.

He agreed and we began to lay the plans. I managed to accumulate a few dollars and couple of makeshift pieces of identification in case I got stopped on the outside. Another friend who worked in the industrial area set up a place where I could hide until nightfall. He also was going to leave me a pair of wire cutters to cut the coiled barbed wire that was on top of the two cyclone fences.

Joe, a good friend of mine, found out what I had planned and asked if he could go with me. He was doing a lot of time and had spent the majority of his life in prison. He was a small, frail man and wore thick, coke-bottle glasses which made his eyes appear to bulge out of their sockets. Without his glasses he was practically blind. I couldn't refuse a friend, so now there were two of us going, which meant two trips through the gate and increased the chance of failure.

When everything was arranged, we waited for a cold, rainy day that would keep the guard in his shack. The day before Thanksgiving, the weather broke cold with a light rain falling from a grey overcast sky. By noon, the wind was blowing the rain across the prison grounds, and I knew if we were going, this would be the day.

Until this point, the escape had been a fantasy—a way to reduce the anger and humiliation of being back in prison. Suddenly, with the plans all set and the right kind of day, the fantasy became reality. Fear that had been pushed to the back of my mind began to tie my stomach into knots. Doubts that had been ignored began to creep to the surface.

What if the guard searches the wheelbarrow?

What if the gun guard sees us from the tower?

What if "Whitey," the inmate who was going to wheel us through the gate, tips the damn thing over?

What if we get trapped in the industrial area and can't get over the fence?

What if they're waiting for us when we go over the fence?

My mind was burning inside with all the "ifs." I felt trapped by my own ingenuity, but I had to go. I had committed myself and couldn't back out.

When I left my cell that day for noon chow, I put on an extra sweatshirt under my prison clothes. I placed the money I'd accumulated in my shoe and had the phoney identification hidden in the lining of my coat.

Joe, my escape partner, was waiting for me in the dining room. "What do you think, man?" he asked in a tense voice.

"If we're going, this is as good a day as we're gonna get," I answered. "Are you ready?"

He nodded his head in the affirmative.

"Have you seen Whitey?" I asked him.

"No," he answered.

We fell into the chow line and picked up our trays. Neither one of us took any of the chow being dished out.

"You better get yourself something to eat, man. We may not get a chance to eat for a while." My voice was low and caring.

Joe shook his head. "Not hungry."

We filled our cups with hot coffee and sat at one of the tables. I had just lifted the metal cup to my lips when I spotted Whitey entering the dining room. He saw us and hurried to our table.

"You guys ready?" he asked. He was a short, stocky man and the yellow rain slicker made him look almost square. He had been in prison all his life and was accustomed to it. He was always scheming to beat the Man. The fact that he might get busted for aiding an escape attempt never entered his mind. It was just one more way to strike back.

"The boss is letting most of the crew off 'cause of the rain." His blond, almost white hair was plastered to his head by the rain. "I told him I wanted to work. We're hauling a bunch of old lumber and tar paper out to the industrial area. Smitty's on the gate and he ain't shook nothin' down all day. The son-of-a-bitch hates the rain."

"What about the set-up for a place to hide once we're in?" I asked.

"No problem," he said. "We got a couple of clothing bins fixed up for you guys to hide in. I'll wheel you out and when I tell you, you haul ass and get in the bin and we'll cover you with dirty coveralls. Sam lifted a pair of wire cutters and hid them in one of the bins."

"When are we going?" Joe asked.

"Now, before it gets any worse outside. The boss wants all of us to quit, but I've got some of the other guys to work until I can get you guys out. Besides, this is a good time 'cause the boss is at lunch."

We waited until Whitey had left the mess hall before we picked up our trays and stacked them at the front of the dining hall.

This is it! I thought. Now or never. There's no turning back.

We left and walked quickly around a corner and down a sidewalk to a large red cell block that was being gutted. There was only one convict besides Whitey in the huge barn-like building. Boards, tar paper, and piles of trash were strewn across the hard clay floor. There were two wheelbarrows next to a large pile of trash.

"Let's go, man. Who's going first?" Whitey asked, looking directly at me.

"I'll go first," I said. It had been my idea and I felt I should be the one to lead.

Whitey spoke to the other con. "You stand guard by the door and I'll cover them up." He turned to me. "I'll take you first and then come back for Joe. Get in this one.'' He pointed to one of the wheelbarrows.

I crawled into the wheelbarrow and pulled my knees up under my chin. Whitey pushed me down farther and rearranged my legs. He then started to pile boards on my body.

"Am I in far enough?'' I asked. The dirt was beginning to trickle down to my face and I felt the urge to sneeze.

"You're okay, you're okay,'' Whitey said.

More boards and then pieces of tar paper were stacked on top of me until the light was gone. I could now feel the boards being tightened down as Whitey tied rope around the pile and the wheelbarrow.

"Okay, Gordy, I'm gonna pick you up. Don't worry about the bumps, and don't make any noise when we get under the guard tower.''

"For chrissakes, don't tip me over!'' I mumbled as we started out. The wheelbarrow tipped precariously as we bumped along. I could hear the rubber tires crunch under the added weight as we moved out of the cell block and onto the sidewalk that led down to the gate. As we rolled along the sidewalk, I could feel the cold November wind and hear the rain splattering on the top boards. My body was wet with perspiration and rain. I could barely breathe.

The ride seemed to go on forever. Then I heard Whitey whisper to me, "We're almost at the gate. Be quiet.''

My heart seemed to be beating loudly enough for them to hear it in downtown Walla Walla. I felt the wheelbarrow being set down.

"What the hell you doin' working in this rain?'' I recognized Smitty's voice.

"Trying to get some of this shit moved.'' Whitey was breathing heavily. "You know how the boss is—he'd work us in a blizzard.''

"Anyone else working?'' Smitty asked.

"Yeah, a couple of other guys, but they're staying in the wing. You know I always get the shit duty.''

"Okay,'' Smitty said. "Go on through.''

I heard the steel bar being drawn and the gate hinges creak as the gate swung open. When Whitey picked the wheelbarrow up to roll through the gate, I felt it tip to the right.

Oh, shit! I almost screamed. Don't tip this son-of-a-bitch over.

Then it was righted and we were moving in a straight line. I breathed a deep, dusty sigh of relief.

"We made it through." I could hear the relief in Whitey's whisper. "We still got a ways to go, so hang in there, Gordy."

I had no choice.

We were on gravel now and the going was a little slower. Damn, that little bastard is strong. He's wheeled me a long way without resting. He's a hell of a dude.

The rain was coming down harder on the boards and it was soaking me. Now that the intense fear was diminishing, the cold was becoming almost unbearable.

The wheelbarrow stopped. "Can you hear me, Gordy?" Whitey asked.

"Yeah, man. Where the hell are we?" My teeth were chattering.

"We're in front of the construction area. I'm gonna untie the rope and unload. When I tell you to get out, you run up the stairs on your left and into the locker room. There's some clothing bins along the wall. Jesse will have one open. You jump in it and we'll cover you with dirty clothes."

I could feel the boards loosening as he untied the rope. "The tower guard can see us, so I gotta wait for him to look inside the joint."

"Okay, man, go!" I felt the boards being thrown off me.

I rolled out of the wheelbarrow onto the wet ground. I stumbled to my feet, trying to adjust my eyes to the light. I saw the stairs and ran up them into a long narrow room. Jesse was standing beside a large bin.

"C'mon, man!" He waved at me frantically.

I jumped into the bin and crouched down. Jesse began throwing dirty, greasy clothes over me and pushing me down farther.

"You stay in there and keep quiet. You've got a couple of hours before they clear the area," he said. "Whitey went back to get Joe. I'll tap on the bin when it's okay to talk." He closed the lid and I could hear his footsteps as he moved away.

It was pitch black in the bin. The air smelled stale and greasy. I didn't have much room to move around. My legs were cramped. The awkward position I was lying in caused pain to shoot through my neck and shoulders. I tried to shift my weight, but it was impossible in the tiny cubicle.

Time dragged on. I could hear people in the room cursing the rain as they changed to dry clothes. Once, the bin was opened and a pair of wet, muddy coveralls was thrown on the stack that covered me. I held my breath. Someone growled, "Don't they ever pick up these damn dirty coveralls. These bins are always full." The lid slammed shut. Then the room was quiet.

I dozed off into a semi-conscious sleep. A light tapping on the bin jerked me awake and back to the reality of where I was.

"You in there, Gordy?" It was Jesse's voice.

"Yeah, man," I choked out. "What's happening?"

"Whitey's got Joe inside. He's waitin' till it's clear," he said.

Then I heard running and a noise that I knew was Joe getting into one of the bins.

There was another tap on my bin. It was Whitey. "Everything went smooth, Gordy. It took longer for Joe 'cause I couldn't get the damn boss to leave. No problem, though. You guys wait till you hear the whistle that the area is clear and then you can come out."

"Thanks, Whitey," I said. "I owe you, man. When we get out and get squared away, I'll take care of you." I felt bad that we were leaving him behind.

"You just beat these bastards. That's all I care about." Whitey tapped on the bin again. "I've gotta split, man. Good luck." I heard him shuffle away and wished that he were going with us.

It became quiet again. I tried to hear Joe in the next bin, but there was no sound except my heart pounding in my ears. We waited. The shrill whistle clearing the area finally sounded. I waited for a few minutes before I pushed the coveralls off me and very slowly lifted the lid of the bin. I peeked out. The room was empty. The light coming from the windows was beginning to fade as the dusk pushed away

the day. I climbed out and went over to the next bin and tapped lightly on it.

"It's clear, Joe. Come on out." I lifted the lid of his bin and
grabbed his searching hand.

"We're out, man. We beat the count. Now, all we gotta do is get
over the fence and we're on our way."

We moved over to one of the windows and crouched down to peer
out. I could see the guard tower that stood between us and freedom.
It sat thirty feet up from the ground on thick, stilt-like legs. A ladder
ran from the ground to a trap door in the floor. I could see the guard
beginning to make his way down the ladder.

"The son-of-a-bitch is leaving," I whispered excitedly.

The guard reached the ground and got into a green Volkswagen
that was parked at the foot of the tower on the outside of the fences.
I felt the excitement build inside me as the car slowly backed onto the
dirt road that circled the institution. I stood up and looked at Joe. In
the dim light his eyes looked huge behind his thick glasses.

"Let's find the wire cutters," I said as we moved over to the bins.
"We'll wait a few minutes before we hit the fence." I was anxious to
get going, but I knew we had to wait for it to get a little darker.

When we'd found the wire cutters, we made our way down the
stairs to the door. There was still a light drizzle, but the wind had
stopped. I nodded to Joe, and we moved slowly along the wall of the
building. We eased our way around the corner until we were directly
across from the tower.

"If we go over the fences right under the tower, we can't be seen
from the other towers," I said to Joe in a hoarse whisper. "I'll climb
the first fence and cut the barbed wire at the top. Then, we can slide
through and drop between the fences and do the same with the second fence. Okay?" Joe nodded.

I crouched down and ran to the first fence at the base of the tower.
My heart was thumping like a piston against my chest. I felt exposed
and could almost hear the bullets slamming into my body. I looked
back at Joe. I could barely see him against the wall.

I put the wire cutters in my back pocket and started climbing the sixteen foot fence. I reached the top, pulled out the wire cutters and started to cut through the coiled barbed wire that was designed to entangle and snare escaping convicts.

There were three strands of wire. I began to twist the first wire in the cutters with one hand while holding onto the fence with the other. Damn, the wire cutters were dull! Who in the hell would leave dull wire cutters, I asked myself. I cursed and twisted until the three strands were cut. I pulled myself up and eased through the opening and climbed down.

I was in the narrow passageway between the two fences. Now I really felt exposed. If anyone came along, there was nowhere to run to hide. Hell, this is no time to think like that! I was only one fence away from freedom!

I turned and motioned to Joe. He ran across to the fence and climbed to the top. He pulled himself awkwardly through the opening and scrambled down to join me in the passageway.

My arms were weak from the strain of hanging onto the fence and fighting the barbed wire. The second fence was shorter, only about ten feet high, but the coiled barbed wire waited at the top.

I turned to Joe. "I'm gonna try to make it through without cutting it this time. These wire cutters are duller than hell. I think if we go over right where the barbed wire hooks to the u-shaped cross arms, we can make it. Okay?"

The rain dripped from his thick glasses as he nodded yes.

I climbed the fence and when I reached the top, I grabbed the metal arms that formed the "u." Carefully I hooked one of my legs on the crossed arm and pulled myself up. When I was on top, I checked to see if I was clear of the coiled wire and jumped. I hit the ground hard with both feet.

I looked around. Everything was quiet except for my heavy breathing. "C'mon, Joe, but be careful and make sure you clear the wire before you jump."

Joe started climbing the fence in a nervous rush. When he reached the top, he struggled to pull himself up. Finally, he was standing on the top ready to jump.

"Okay, man, jump," I said, "but be sure you . . ." Before I could finish, Joe jumped. There was a grinding sound of metal on metal, a ripping sound as Joe snapped to a halt, hanging upside down by one leg on the outside of the fence.

"Goddam, I told you to clear!" I spat out.

I reached and jerked his body to free his leg. He screamed in pain as the metal barbs ripped his leg. "My leg's got a noose around it," he moaned.

I looked around apprehensively. My first thought was to leave Joe hanging in the wire and take off. But I had a reputation to think of. What if he survived and went back inside and told all my partners that I had run off and left him? What would they think of me then? Damn! Why did this have to happen now when we were so close?

I knew I had to try to lift him up to take his weight off the entrapped leg, but I was too weak to climb back up the fence. We couldn't stay in this spot much longer because the guard from #3 tower could see us if he decided to look this way. It was supper time and the guard would be concentrating on the chow line. But if he checked the industrial area . . .

The only thing to do was somehow get the weight off the wire so I could break it with the dull wire cutters. There was a hay barn about a hundred feet from the fence. I ran over and looked around. There were stacks of baled hay in the barn.

I picked one of the smaller bales up, stumbled back to where Joe was hanging and placed it under him. He could touch it with his hands.

"Look, Joe," I said in whispered desperation, "I'm going to get another bale and put it on top of this one and climb up and try to cut you loose. You gotta' help me lift your weight off that leg. Okay?"

"Okay. But hurry. This damn thing is tearing my leg up," he moaned.

I ran over to the barn again and brought back another bale and placed it on top of the first. My heart was pounding and I was gasping for air as I climbed up on top of the bales of hay. I told Joe to help me get his weight on my shoulders. He did with painful groans.

"Quiet, man, the tower will hear you," I whispered.

When he had his body balanced on my shoulders, I eased myself up to a standing position. His weight almost made me fall, but I grabbed the fence for balance. I held the fence with one hand and took the wire cutters out of my pocket. The barbed wire that was snagged on his leg was slack and I could hook the cutters in it. I began to twist and turn the cutters, working them back and forth. I could feel the wire beginning to weaken.

Damn the guy who brought these dull cutters; with good ones we wouldn't be in this fix, I cursed to myself.

Finally the wire broke. I released Joe's weight and he fell, rolling off the bales of hay and landing in the wet gravel at the foot of the fence. I jumped off the bales and helped him to his feet. I was weak and tired. The ordeal of climbing the fences, carrying the bales of hay, holding Joe's weight on my shoulders, and fearing that at any minute we would be shot by the tower guard had drained me.

I helped Joe release the barbed noose from around his torn and bleeding leg. I grabbed him by the arm and we ran out into the muddy wheat field that surrounded the prison. We ran about fifty yards and plopped down behind a mound to rest. I looked up at the sky. The cold drops of rain washed the perspiration from my face.

"God, it's good to be out of that stinking joint," I said.

I looked at Joe's leg. It was bleeding and a raw red welt circled his thin white ankle. I asked him how it felt and if he could walk all right. He said it hurt like hell, but there was no way that it was going to stop him.

I suddenly realized where we were. We had escaped! We were out! But what next? Where to go? All I could see were plowed wheat fields, muddy and dismal in the rainy evening light.

"We got to put some miles between us and the joint, man," I said to no one in particular. "They're gonna be after us soon as they take the nine o'clock count." I turned to Joe. "Let's go."

I started to get up when Joe grabbed my arm. "I can't," he said.

"What the hell you mean you can't?" I asked.

"I lost my glasses back at the fence. You know I can't see a damn thing without them. I gotta go back and get 'em.''

I looked up to the heavens and swore to myself.

Knowing that he was in no shape to go back, I said in painful resignation, "I'll go. You wait here."

"Thanks, Gordy," he said weakly. "I think they're probably by the bales. They must have come off when I fell."

"I'll find them." And with that, I jumped up and wove my way back towards the fence.

When I was about fifty feet from the fence, I crouched down and looked around. Everything was quiet. The bales were standing next to the fence. I rushed over to the bales and bent down to look for Joe's glasses. At first I couldn't find them, son-of-a-bitch, then I spotted them half submerged in the muck a couple of feet from one of the bales. I picked them up and hurried back to where Joe was waiting.

Together we headed across the uneven, furrowed fields away from the dimming lights of the state prison. It was tough going because of the heavy mud sticking to our ankle high boots. After a hundred yards, the boots felt like they were made of lead. We would stop every so often to scrape off the thick, clay-like mud, then trudge on through the night.

I kept listening for some sign that they were after us. The only sounds in the still night were the slurping of our footsteps and the patter of rain on wet ground.

Buildings began to take form in the distance as daylight broke over the wet muddy land. We had walked all night.

Twice we dove for cover when headlights stabbed through the darkness. I knew that there had to be patrols out searching for us because the roads we were crossing were seldom traveled at night. I also knew that when daylight came, the air patrols that they used to search for escapees could spot us easily.

During a rest stop, I turned to Joe and said, "When it gets daylight, man, we'd better dig us a hole to hide in because there ain't gonna be no cover in these fields if they send out search planes."

Joe looked cold and miserable. As we started out again after the brief rest, he lifted one mud-laden foot and placed it tiredly in front of the other. His torn leg didn't seem to be bothering him, or if it did, he wasn't complaining. We trudged along another mile or so, and after climbing a small rolling hill, we spotted a barn-like building in a small draw off to our left.

"Hey, man, let's hide in that barn during the daylight hours and travel when it gets dark again," Joe's voice pleaded.

We turned and headed for the barn. New energy pumped through my aching body. The barn looked like it was used to store surplus hay. We pushed open the heavy sliding doors and went inside. The place had a stale, musty smell but it was dry and filled with loosely stacked hay. We dug a couple of holes in the hay and lay down, burrowing deep inside the dry chaffed hay. The warm covering gradually eased the coldness from my tired body and I dozed off into a fitful sleep.

The day wore on. Once, we were awakened by the sound of an airplane cruising overhead. I whispered to Joe that it was probably a search plane looking for us. There was nothing we could do but try to go back to sleep. It was difficult to rest because every nerve in my body was aching with tension. Even the rustling of the mice or rats as they scurried through the building made me jump.

"What time do you think it is, Joe?"

"I don't know, but it must be past noon. My stomach's growling like hell."

His comment reminded me that I hadn't eaten for over thirty hours. I hadn't thought about food, but I realized I was hungry. "We've got to get a car and get out of this part of the country. We should be close to Waitsburg. I saw some farms not too far away. Maybe we can steal a car from one of them when it gets dark."

Another plane was passing overhead. It sounded low.

"That must be another search plane. Where do you think we should go?"

Joe's question made me face the reality of our situation. We had escaped, but we had made no plans beyond getting over the fences and away from the prison. We had eleven dollars between us and nowhere to go.

I spoke my thoughts to Joe. "We can't go to Seattle, 'cause that's the first place they're gonna go looking for us. Spokane is out, 'cause I just got convicted there. I know a woman in Missoula, Montana. If we can get there, she'd put us up for awhile 'till we can figure something out."

It was easier not to face the truth. My mind was blanking out the fact that the only way for us to survive was to pull a caper. We needed to get enough money to get out of this part of the country. It wasn't going to be easy because they would have every law enforcement officer around looking for us. There'd be news bulletins with our descriptions and all the farmers would be alerted.

"Man, we should've had someone pick us up or something." Joe's voice projected his realization that we hadn't planned beyond the walls.

12. The Convict Code

After the short-lived escape had ended in capture, Walla Walla became my home, my way of life. I didn't like it, although there was significant personal gratification in being accepted and in beating the Man. The inmates who had "grown up" with me began to expect certain behavior and support for their actions, whether good or bad. The pressures to meet these expectations were a burden, but something that I needed to give me a sense of self-esteem.

I'd become a capable leader in this abnormal society. The "convict code" had become my creed. I lived by code. I prided myself on the reputation I'd developed as a "good convict." The prison guards understood the "convict code" and patterned their dealings with inmates accordingly. An experienced prison guard would never put an inmate in the position of being suspected of snitching or fraternizing with staff. They knew the inmate power bases and the inmate leaders and used this knowledge to manage the population.

The reputation and identity that I'd established in those early years trapped me in an existence that became a prison in itself. I was expected to behave in certain ways by my peers, by the prison staff, and by law enforcement. Once expectations are established, change becomes a threat to all those who know you. "Don't try to con the con—you're a thief and a wrong-doer. Don't give me that shit about straightening your life out.'' Words like these made up the general feedback you received from your peers if you tried to break out of this mental prison.

Your present behavior is judged by your past and the Man sees it as "running a game" if you try to act differently. Many try, but few are able to make the break. The pressures are too great and old habits too firmly entrenched.

The years in prison slowly change your picture of reality. Every day you learn more about how to survive, how to beat the Man and how to gain acceptance in the prison society. As your knowledge and skills increase, the basic principles of right and wrong begin to fade and are replaced by a new set of rules, the "convict code." Just like any social structure, the values and accepted behavior are established by the most experienced, the seniors. In a prison it's the old con, the one who has done the most time, or the "baddest," the one who is most feared, who sets the standards.

The Man has little ability to impact this social structure. There is minimal contact between inmate and staff and what contact there is centers around conflict and hostility. The majority of prison staff members operate from a philosophy that suggests that inmates are basically untrustworthy, lazy and dishonest. Most inmates hold similarly ingrained attitudes about staff. They believe that staff members are out to get inmates, that they will set inmates up and that they can't be trusted. It is within this environment that correctional professionals attempt to bring about constructive change in behavior. It is no surprise that there have not been significant results from our correctional system. The changes that occur are all inconsistent with society's norms. The knowledge acquired in prison increases dishonesty, manipulation and hostility toward authority.

The idea of segregating lawbreakers from society is still our most effective protection against crime. Citizens have the right to expect their persons and their property to be safe from predators. Yet the very fact that we place a person in prison may be the exact reason that person doesn't change in positive ways. And since we have no ability to set up a controlled environment upon release from prison, the inmate who has slowly developed the ability to survive in prison becomes less capable of surviving on "the streets." The more time he does, the less likely he is to succeed outside. He becomes a part of the revolving door, a repeater who does life on the installment plan.

Over the years there have been significant shifts in society's attitudes about how to deal with inappropriate behavior. The pendulum swings from right to left. First, the guiding principle is "swift and sure" punishment, the "spare the rod and spoil the child" theory. Then the movement shifts to the "Dr. Spock approach" of positive reinforcement, warm fuzzies and unconditional love. All approaches are designed as "cure-alls" of some form or another. These societal shifts encompass child rearing, management styles, dealing with disadvantaged groups and treatment of lawbreakers and the inmates in our prisons.

The late sixties and early seventies caught society in a rapid swing. We were in an era of social soul cleansing. Racial minorities were heightening the awareness of discrimination. Sit-ins, freedom marches and riots were bringing the issue into middle-class America's living rooms. Equality and justice for all became the political strategy. People began actively seeking out a "cause" that they could rally around.

This awareness of people's inhumanity to people and our need to atone for our past transgressions somehow transferred to society's treatment of convicted felons. The convict suddenly became one focal point of people looking for a cause. Where could you find someone who needed love and understanding more than the inmate in prison? It was the time of the political prisoner, the George Jackson Brigade and self-government.

The joint had been changing and it was becoming more and more difficult to do time. Drugs, homosexuality, and racial conflicts created a dangerous environment. The new breed of inmate was more apt to stick you with a shank or form gangs that operated almost like terrorists, ripping off the weaker convicts. An environment was created where survival became the uppermost thing in the minds of most of the population.

For my first fifteen years in prisons, most beefs were settled by the two inmates involved. They would go behind the cell blocks and settle their differences with fists. But now stabbings were a common occurrence and you could lose your life over a carton of cigarettes or a five dollar paper of heroin. The older convicts had withdrawn from the leadership roles that had stabilized the inmate population and members of the new breed had taken over. Their values were different. The "convict code" had been eroded by drugs. Racial groups had formed for self-protection. The sense of brotherhood that had existed within the Walls had been replaced by a sense of fear. The fear and hostility transferred subtly to the correctional staff, and the distance between staff and inmates had become wider and more difficult to cross.

When I returned to Walla Walla the last time, a new director of corrections had been appointed. He was a psychiatrist with an extensive background in mental health, but minimal experience in prisons and virtually no experience in dealing with maximum security prisons like Walla Walla. Every new director or warden immediately begins to consider change. "It's not working. How can I make it work?" Some of the Scandinavian countries were having fantastic success with an innovative approach to prison management that centered around self-government, transferring responsibility to the inmate and allowing a governing body of convicts to make decisions. The warden of Walla Walla was sent on a fact-finding mission to explore this concept firsthand. Upon his return, and after what seemed a minimal amount of study, the director issued an order. "We are going to throw out all rules. Inmates will elect a governing body and we will have self-government at Washington State Penitentiary." What followed was utter chaos. It would have been humorous except for the inmates and staff who were subjected to brutality and anarchy. This clumsy experiment with human lives failed miserably.

The institutions where self-government had been successful were small, one-hundred-man institutions. Walla Walla had over one thousand of the state's toughest convicts. In the institutions where self-government had worked, the concept had been well thought out and the staff had been involved in and committed to the project. At Walla Walla it was introduced with no preparation and no staff support. The ideas were violently opposed.

As a result of the inadequate preparation that had been made for the new concept, the institution was on the brink of anarchy. The concept of self-government had just been introduced. The ideas were being shoved down the throats of the prison guards. They had retaliated by taking a hands-off attitude. "If they're going to govern themselves, then let them take care of their own problems." They had not only abrogated their authority, they were actively working to undermine the self-government concept. Small bands of inmate predators began to roam the institution. Robberies, beatings and stabbings became commonplace. The weak, the old, the less sophisticated became the prey.

I'd gotten married when I was on the streets. My wife Janie, her child Tami, and our tiny Tina were living downtown on welfare. Janie was pregnant, and every Saturday when they'd come to visit me, it ripped me up inside. I really didn't like myself very much anymore. I needed to get out. I felt a deep sense of guilt at leaving her alone, now pregnant and with two young daughters, to exist on welfare while I played big shot in the penitentiary. How could I have brought these special people into my world and then left them to suffer because of me? I knew it bothered Janie, but she never complained. Her faith in me gave me added strength, and I struggled to find a way to speed up my release.

Because of my wife and daughters and my desire to get out of prison as soon as possible, I didn't want to get involved. I knew you could lose your life with even the slightest provocation. I wanted out. I wanted to turn my head and ignore the bullying and brutality. But I had too many friends, saw too many people who were being mentally and physically beaten by the environment, to ignore this madness that was encompassing me.

Racial tensions increased in the prison, fanned by the hostile, predominantly white correctional staff. Black and white conflicts mounted. Beatings and robberies began taking on racial tones.

Racial groups began to isolate themselves, forming individual political cliques designed to protect their people from the growing insanity. The blacks united behind the Black Prisoners' Forum, the Indians banded together and became the United Indians of All Tribes, the chicanos followed suit with a chicano organization and the white population solidified behind The Lifers' Club and a loose-knit white brotherhood group. The prison became a powder keg. Every incident became a racial issue, with retaliation by the racial groups involved almost certain.

My reputation over the years had crossed racial lines. I had always been fair and a supporter of the underdog. My circle of friends included leaders from every group in the prison. It became increasingly difficult to remain passive. Daily conflicts accelerated in number and intensity. I was being called on more and more often to act as a mediator in the racial conflicts.

The pending confrontation between racial groups finally exploded. I can't recall now which of the petty incidents triggered the explosion. I found myself thrown into the middle of the chaos. An arrangement was made between black and white leaders to meet in the prison auditorium and "settle" things once and for all. Four hundred inmates armed with knives, clubs, iron bars and baseball bats began to slowly assemble in the dingy, dimly lit auditorium.

There was no attempt by the prison staff to stop the confrontation. They knew it was destined to be a bloody, brutal struggle between human beings, a senseless slaughter. These men would "stick" another human being because of the color of his skin. Guards kept to their "hands off" policy. It was first degree insanity. A number of my long time friends and partners, both black and white, were lining up, taking stands that could lead to their own death or the forced killing of another person.

The auditorium was full of hostile, silent, armed convicts waiting for the "kick off." The prison guards, after the convicts had assembled, had locked the auditorium doors and left the institution. Staff felt this would be the final blow needed to end self-government once and for all. "These people are animals. How can they govern themselves?'' It was insane, but prisons are a breeding ground for insanity.

As I looked around the auditorium, I saw black guys who were good guys, friends of mine, who in a minute would be forced to kill me because I was white. I saw white guys who would attack blacks because they were black. Interspersed throughout both groups, I saw the predators, the instigators, men who were filled with hate, their faces gleaming with the sick excitement of the pending battle.

Someone had to put an end to this. I couldn't allow myself to stand by and let it happen without attempting to stop this senseless destruction. I walked slowly up the narrow stairs to the center of the stage at the front of the auditorium. My heart was pounding and I felt alone and vulnerable. I looked out over the mass of angry, hostile faces, black on one side, white on the other. I began. ''What the hell are we doing? Here we are down in this stinking auditorium about to kill each other because we are white or black. The Man has locked the doors and said let the animals prove how responsible they are, that they can govern themselves. Boy, we're going to show them aren't we? Hell, I look around at guys who are my friends, guys who've escaped with me, drunk with me and raised hell with me and because I'm white, they're ready to stick a knife in me. What the hell's goin' on? This ain't no way to solve our problems.'' The men were beginning to look at each other. I could sense the tension easing.

A huge barrel-chested black guy, a friend even though we didn't spend a lot of time together, separated from the blacks and climbed the stairs to stand beside me. He was one of the ''baddest'' dudes in the joint and a leader among the blacks. ''Gordy's right, brothers. This ain't no solution. We're playing right into the Man's hands. They put us against each other and they just sit out there and laugh.'' Other leaders were beginning to join us on the stage. I knew it was over, for now.

''Let's put our knives and weapons in a barrel when we leave. Someone set up a couple of those fifty-gallon drums at the door and just dump them in as we leave. We need to form a race relations committee so when there's a problem between races, we can bring it to the committee and let them deal with the issue. How many of you think we should form a race relations committee? Raise your hand." All but a few of the inmates raised their hands. "No jumping on guys and no retaliation until the committee has had a chance to act. Each group pick two people that you respect."

The guards, sensing that the confrontation was over, opened the auditorium doors. Men began to file through. You could hear the clanging of metal as knives and steel bars were dumped in the barrels. When everyone was gone, I turned to Johnnie, the black leader who had been first to support me, and reached for his hand. "Thanks, man. I needed you real bad." I shook hands with the others who had joined us on the stage. "We've got to form the race relations committee and stop this insanity." The two fifty-gallon barrels were full of knives, bars, clubs, ice picks, chains.

A tall stooped lifer spoke up. "Man, this place would have been a blood bath if this thing had broke loose." We picked the barrels up and carried them to the guard's control booth and set them down without a word. There was a startled look of disbelief on his face as we walked away. We were forced into the role of establishing some form of control. The race relations committee was formed. Representatives were chosen by majority election by each racial group. There was no more "doing my own time." Things had changed for me somehow; even then, I could sense the turning point.

Day and night we were called on to quell disturbances. We established a drunk tank where we could take inmates who were under the influence of drugs or alcohol, a place where they could dry out. We ran continuous sessions with potential troublemakers, and when all else failed, we would resort to physical force. A loose sense of order began to return to the institution.

There was minimal support from line staff. Except for the warden and two or three of his executive staff, we were on our own. They were caught in the same situation as the inmate population. Self-government had been mandated by the director of corrections. There was no turning back. The rule book had been thrown out. The inmates were to establish their own rules and rewrite the book.

I learned a great deal about conflict resolution, leadership and decision making in that short nine months. I learned that one thousand inmates confined in a maximum security prison, many of whom have never been able to govern their lives in a free environment, have little chance of establishing a workable government inside prison. I learned that change is a gradual process that needs to be implemented with the support of the people responsible for making it work. I learned that once you give up turf or decision-making responsibility, it is difficult to take those things back, even in the confines of a prison. I learned a great deal more about people. There are good and bad people, humane and inhumane people in all groups. It has nothing to do with the color of a person's skin or his position in life. I realized that you either learn to live together or your life has little value.

I began to see that wrong is wrong and that you can't condone wrong just because the person who commits the act is your friend. I began to separate myself from the prison mentality that had controlled my life for so many years. I didn't know how, but I knew I wasn't going to do any more time.

Within a few months I'd managed to get transferred to the minimum security building. This moved me outside the Walls and increased my freedoms. Because of the time I had left on my five year sentence, Bob Rhay, the warden, had to personally sign my minimum custody status. He knew I wouldn't violate his trust, and because Janie was pregnant, he agreed to allow me to move to the minimum security building.

The building had no bars, fences or walls. Security was a mental thing. Most of the men at minimum security were near their release dates. Inmates in the minimum security building were allowed more visits than those incarcerated "inside." There were guidelines to follow and they knew that a violation of the rules or an escape attempt would mean a trip back inside the Walls and more time added to their prison sentences. The price for breaking the rules was high.

The pressures, however, were less at the minimum security

building. Self-government created a different sort of management problem. The problems were similar to those faced by supervisors in industry. How do you motivate people to work without the ability to reward and punish? In order to govern or manage effectively, the governing body has to have the power to reward and punish. This power still was in the hands of the administration. Therefore, the government was seen by many inmates as a tool of the administration. Inmates were not required to work. There was no penalty clause for those who chose not to work. There was minimal reward for those who did. Gradually the maintenance of the institution began to deteriorate. Living quarters were left unattended. The kitchen crew lost interest and the kitchen deteriorated. Meals were often served late and half-cooked. The crops of hay and vegetables were harvested late or sometimes not at all. "Why work? Hell, you get out of prison just as fast and there ain't no money in it. Might as well lay on your ass" was the response of many inmates.

As president of the inmate government, it was my responsibility to motivate people to work. Getting men to cut, rake, bale and load hay in the 100 degree Walla Walla heat was one of the major challenges. Somehow we had to get men to volunteer. I decided that first the inmate government had to be part of the volunteer work force. We met, and I convinced the other members to join me in volunteering. Then we met with the warden to negotiate some form of reward. We settled on an extra movie each week and allowing the inmates at minimum security building to have evening visits. Prior to that time, an inmate could only have visits on weekends and holidays. The warden agreed to our proposal, and we took back something that would help all the inmates. We also decided that the hours we worked should be flexible as long as we got the hay in the barn on time. The result was that we had the hay in the barn more quickly than ever before. Contests between inmate crews developed to see who could put more loads in the barn. Winners were rewarded with time off or a special dinner.

This experience taught me the power of leadership by example. It supported the idea that given proper incentives and treated with respect, men are motivated to do what is right. With some ability to reward and punish, self-government can exist in a minimum security institution where predators and fear are not dominant. Given support of management and staff, this concept can instill positive behavioral changes in men. Implementation of the concept needed constant monitoring and guidance, but given the above ingredients, self-government could be an effective correctional process.

The responsibilities that I was forced to accept during this period of time strengthened my resolve to stay out. Janie knew the pressures I was under in the prison. Visits would be interrupted by a call for me to settle some confrontation or to talk someone out of stabbing a fellow inmate. She understood. She knew I had to help. She had become a vital part of my life.

13. Husband, Father, Convict

I had met Janie in a most unusual setting. Her uncle was serving one of his many prison terms in the state penitentiary. Over the past fifteen years her Uncle Bob (referred to by friends as the "Speckled Bird") and I had walked hundreds of miles around the yard at Walla Walla. We'd spent many hours discussing the most effective ways to open the safes of unsuspecting "square johns." Both of us were in the minimum security building, about to be released and confident that we'd gotten "slicker" and would never get busted again. By now I was a four time loser and had become a professional convict and a leader within the Walls.

I was in the prison mess hall one morning when the Speckled Bird joined me. After cursing the food and coffee and giving a vivid description of one of the guard's ancestors, Bob turned to me. "I got a visit today. My niece is coming over from Spokane."

There were four of us at the breakfast table and one of my partners jokingly remarked, "Man, you don't get visits. Who the hell would visit you?"

"Hey, that's great! You ought to stay in from work and clean your ass up!" one of the other guys laughed. "Hell, let me visit her. She ain't going to want to talk about cracking safes." The joking continued.

Bob hadn't had a visit for as long as I could remember. His life was the Washington State Penitentiary. All his friends were here. He was a convict's convict, totally loyal to the "convict code." Anyone who didn't belong to that world he rejected as a lousy "square john." I really hadn't considered the idea that he might know someone who wasn't a thief. Bob looked at me. "If you're around the building when she shows up, come on in the visiting room and I'll introduce you. She's a 'jam up' broad and you'll like her."

I had no free-world contacts, and the women who over the years had entered my life were after excitement and thrills. When I'd get busted, which was quite regularly, these women would just find someone else before nightfall.

I told Bob that I would stop in for a minute if I got the chance and I walked away. My mind was on "the streets." I was down to three days before my release and I was scared. I'd been out three or four times and had never stayed out for very long. A year had been my longest run; one time I had been out only thirty days.

Inside the Walls I was "somebody." Everybody looked up to me. You don't mess with Gordy, man. He's bad! I had an identity. People cared about me inside the Walls. I was the president of the Inmate Council, a group that represented the inmate population, and quarterback on the "Stealers," the joint football team. I either held or had held, all the boxing titles at Walla Walla, from middleweight to heavyweight.

Over the years I had become a product of the institutional environment. Whenever I was released, I felt out of place . . . like God had left a part out. I was incomplete.

I envied those people who lived in that other world. I could never figure out how to achieve a productive, honest life on the "outside." I'd never had a job. I always felt that if I could find a good job, I would stay out. But these were penitentiary dreams created in the Walt Disney world of prison. You can't get a job without skills, not only work skills, but social skills. I belonged to an abnormal society, a sub-culture. But deep inside I knew that I was not a bad person. I cared about people and wanted to be different, but I didn't know how.

It was one o'clock in the afternoon. I'd finished my job of supervising the cleaning of the inmate dining room. I was standing in the central control area where inmates reported for work assignments, mail, visits, or other institution activities, when Bob, the Speckled Bird, walked by on his way to the visiting room. "Janie's here. Stop by for a minute." He sounded anxious.

"Okay, man, I'll stop in and say hello, but the Man's starting to bust guys for being in the visiting room when they don't have visits."

"You know they ain't going to say nothing to you! Come on." He disappeared through the door that led into the visiting area.

I hadn't had a visit for a year or so and felt awkward about busting in on someone I didn't even know. It's important to Bob, I thought, so I'd better do it.

I walked by the window that opened into the visiting room. I glanced in and saw Bob with his niece on the other side of the room in the corner. There were only two or three other inmates having visits, so it didn't look too bad. I looked around to see where the lieutenant was. He was in his office with the door closed. The guard on the desk was a friend of mine and I knew he wouldn't say anything. I pushed the door open and walked over to where they were seated. Bob looked up excitedly. "I want you to meet Janie, my niece. This is Gordy Graham. I've told you about him. He's a good friend of mine."

"Hi. How you doing? Don't believe everything the Speckled Bird tells you." She's young. Can't be over twenty, I thought. She had light brown hair and seemed tiny and helpless beside her uncle, who was a big man, gnarled and hardened by years in the penitentiary. She had a pretty face generously sprinkled with freckles. You could see they were related. Bob's nickname, the Speckled Bird, came from the freckles that covered his face and hands.

She looked at me and smiled a little crooked smile that sent shivers through my body. "I'm glad to meet you. Bob's talked a lot about you. He said you're getting out in a few days." Her voice was relaxed and made me feel comfortable.

"Three more days and I'm giving this place back to them. Where do you live?"

"I've just moved downtown." She seemed to be friendly, so I thought I'd take a chance and see if she might be interested in meeting me when I got out.

"Why don't I stop by when I get released and you and me could take a trip through Oregon. It would give us a chance to get to know each other." She didn't react too well to this suggestion. In her own way she told me to "stuff it!" Well, I messed that up real good, I thought, as I walked out of the visiting room. I could feel her eyes following me.

I went back to my room and lay down on the bunk. She's a nice person. I like her. How the hell do you get to know someone who isn't a hustler? The only women I had ever been involved with were thieves or hustlers. You just laid your game down, and if it was right, they'd become your "old lady."

I wanted to see her again. I decided I could find out where she lived and contact her when I got out. My mind was busy imagining ways to get her to see me again. Hopefully, I could make a better impression next time around.

The next three days passed slowly. Hours seemed like days and the nights were months. The morning of my release, I got up early, packed my few belongings, and made my way to the inmate dining room. My partners were gathered at our regular table, waiting for me. Steam from the huge silver coffee urn drifted toward the ceiling. The fresh smell of coffee filled the mess hall. Inmates kept coming over to our table, wishing me luck, offering words of advice on how to stay out.

I felt a sense of sorrow in leaving all these guys behind. They were my friends and cared about me. "I wish I could take you guys with me, but you'll be out soon and we'll all have a party in Seattle." We all knew that it would never happen—survival was too tough—but the desire and emotions were real.

The dining room was full now of inmates preparing for another day's existence. Poor bastards. I'd be in Seattle by noon. I was nervous and anxious to get started. It was 7:45 a.m. The driver would be here to pick me up at eight o'clock and take me to the main institution. I would sign release papers, pick up my forty dollars gate money and my bus ticket to Seattle. I glanced up as the conversation at the table suddenly stopped. Withers, a guard, was heading for our table. He was a real canine, continuously finding ways to make life miserable for the inmates. There were a lot of guards who did their job and busted you if you got out of line. You could live with that. But Withers was a different breed. He hated convicts and always looked for ways to mess up their lives.

"What's that son-of-a-bitch want?" someone growled.

Withers stopped at our table and in a voice that carried through the dining room ordered, "Okay, Graham, let's go up there and clean your room. Roll up your mattress and bring it downstairs to the clothing room."

He'd never messed with me before. He knew I was leaving and it was his last opportunity to let me know I wasn't quite out of prison. He had one last chance to exert his authority in front of the other inmates.

"Hey, man, I'm leaving. The driver will be here in a few minutes, and besides, I don't have a room. That place belongs to the state!" The anger in my voice rose to a high pitch.

He swelled with authority. "You ain't going nowhere till that room is clean. You aren't released until you sign your release papers, and until then you're still a convict! Let's go!"

"Man, I ain't cleanin' no goddam room. I'm not sweeping, mopping or rolling no mattress, and you better get the hell away from my table!" Anger had exploded in my head. The tension and frustration of years of failure welled up in me. I stood up from the table and stuck my face right in his. "You better not mess with me. I'm getting out of this joint, and you stay off my case. Just leave me alone. I mean it!" My voice shook with emotion. Wither's face was white and I could see the fear in his eyes.

My partners were trying to calm me down. "Come on, man, you're getting out. Don't let some lousy guard mess you up! We'll clean your room, man.''

"Hey, Withers, we'll get his mattress and sweep his room." The Speckled Bird and a couple of other inmates hurried from the dining room and headed for my room.

"Okay, Graham, I'm going to give you a pass this time, but don't come back!" He seemed relieved and anxious to get out of the situation he had created. I sat down at the table. The realization of what I had done suddenly hit me. My body was weak from the violent outburst, and I had to fight back tears of relief.

"Shit, I almost blew my release date, man. That son-of-a-bitch had to mess with me." My voice was quiet now, the fun and excitement of the morning were gone. The stark reality of prison had erased all joy with the awareness that freedom could be snatched away at the whim of one sadistic bastard like Withers.

"Man, I'm never coming back! I don't think I could do another jolt." I stood up and shook hands with all my friends. The mood was somber now, each of them wishing he were in my shoes. Each of them hoping that I would make it . . . this time.

Bob and the others who had gone to clean my room were back. "Man, there wasn't anything on the floor. All we had to do was bring your mattress down." They sounded disgusted.

"Thanks, you guys. I lost my damn temper. The son-of-a-bitch was trying to prove some goddam thing, using me as an example."

I stood up and they joined me as we walked to the front of the building where the inmate driver was waiting. We shook hands and I got into the blue station wagon. I waved back to the small group of inmates waving and shouting final words of advice.

The tremendous feeling of excitement was dampened by the deep sorrow I felt. I hated leaving people I cared about stuck in that world filled with hate, anger and helplessness. I turned my eyes to the front and thought to myself, I'll never come back to this lousy stinking joint.

When I hit the streets, I immediately began to seek out my old haunts. It wasn't long before I was involved in my habitual illegal activities. The memories of Janie kept coming back. The pretty face with the little crooked smile wouldn't leave me alone. I wanted to see her again.

I found out that she was living in a small town near Walla Walla and had gone to work in a lounge. For the next few weeks, I drove the six hundred miles from Seattle to Walla Walla so many times I lost count. Each time I did my best to convince her that she should return to Seattle with me. For the first time in my life, I was in love. Janie finally weakened and consented to give it a try. We lived together for a year before we were married. Janie brought Tami to the family and then our tiny Tina was born.

My life style hadn't changed. I was still stealing but trying hard to be careful. The pressure was tremendous but I couldn't quit. I didn't know anything else. I could sense Janie's fear, but I kept reassuring her that nothing would happen. I'd had two or three close calls and each time I became more cautious. I moved away from town to avoid the ex-convicts who kept seeking me out to borrow money or to get me to be a part of some "get rich" scheme. I knew I was living on borrowed time, but I kept telling myself and Janie that after the next caper I would quit. But there always seemed to be something that would happen and it would be just one more. Some old partner who needed money, or a lawyer or bondsman who needed to be paid.

Janie and I had moved to a little five acre place about thirty miles from Seattle. One of my old partners had just been paroled and, as usual, he was broke when he hit town and needed money. I hadn't pulled a caper for a couple of weeks, so my bank roll was slim, but I wanted to help him out. There was a fence who dealt in stolen coin collections and jewelry. He lived on Magnolia Hill, an upperclass neighborhood in Seattle. I knew that he had a square-doored safe in his basement where he kept his coin collections and whatever jewelry he had on hand. I'd never touched it, but I always knew it was there. It was like a savings account I could draw on if times got tough! When Ed hit town, I decided it was time to withdraw my money.

There was a convention in town and I knew the fence was going to be there. It was the fall of the year and darkness came early to Seattle. We loaded our tools into my 1964 Chevrolet convertible. Before we left home, we called the fence's house six or seven times and let the phone ring for at least a minute. There was no answer. I knew he was at the convention, but I wanted to take every precaution.

We drove to a convenient place and parked our car a block from the immaculate, split-level home that sat on a corner lot overlooking the lights of the city. We sat in the car for a few minutes, watching the house. The night was silent, only a light misty rain disturbing the peaceful tranquility of this affluent alien neighborhood. Two main streets that ran down either side of the hill were our only escape routes. We'd determined that going down across a long bridge over a navy yard was the fastest and safest route to travel. We checked the walkie-talkies one last time. Ed and I walked quickly down the tree-covered sidewalk and slipped quietly in amongst the finely manicured shrubbery beside the impressive home. We watched silently for some time. The house was dark. I knew it would be a quick easy job and we could be home within an hour. I took out a small pipe wrench that I intended to use to break the lock on the door. I checked the 32 automatic that I had tucked in the waist of my pants.

"Okay, Ed, I'll open the door. You keep an eye out for anyone walking on the sidewalks. When we get inside, you stay in the living room. I'll take the tools and go downstairs to the study. Stay by the front window where you can watch the streets. If anyone comes, let me know. When they're gone, signal me and I'll go back to work. It will only take me a few minutes to peel the safe, and we can get the hell out of here!"

We moved silently across the dark lawn up a short staircase to the front door, shielded from the street by overhanging vines of ivy. I placed the pipe wrench on the door knob and twisted it until I heard the lock snap. I turned, handed the wrench to Ed and pushed against the door. It swung open. I stopped for a moment, listening. The room was dark and silent. I stepped through the open doorway and as I did, the 32 slipped. As I pulled it out and turned to hand it to Ed, a blast exploded in my ears and two violent streaks of flame shot from the darkness. I felt the hot searing pain as my left leg was ripped from under me.

"Son-of-a-bitch! We've been set up, man," I screamed. "Get out of here!" I dove out the door and rolled down the marble stairs. I came to my feet running. I could feel the blood running down my leg, but fear had locked out any pain. We reached the car. "Ed, you drive, man. I don't know how bad I'm hit!"

Ed started the car. He threw it into gear and let the clutch out with a jerk. The motor coughed and died. He had killed the motor. "Shit, man, we're going to get busted up here. Get this son-of-a-bitch going!" Again he killed the motor. Finally on the third try, we went leap-frogging down the street. When we pulled onto the long bridge that spanned a large naval yard and industrial area, Ed had the car pretty well under control. As we neared the center of the bridge, all the cop cars in the world came screeching to a halt, blocking our exit. I glanced out the back window. Police cars, with blue lights flashing, had shut off the hillside behind us.

"What the hell we gonna' do, man?" Ed's voice sounded panicky. He'd only been out of the joint for four days.

"Well, it's 350 feet down to the deck, we can't jump, and I sure as hell ain't going to shoot it out with a 32 and a pen knife! We'll just have to try to bluff our way through." Ed pulled off the end of the bridge into the army of blue-uniformed police officers. Three or four were in civilian clothes, and I knew we were in serious trouble. With twenty-odd guns pointing in the direction of our car, they invited us to get out. We climbed out into the waiting arms of the officers, who assisted us in assuming a familiar position with hands flat against the car's soft canvas top.

They'd been dealing with both of us for years, and a detective who knew me asked, "What's going on? There's been reports of gunfire from this area."

"Hell, I don't know. We're just driving around!" My voice didn't sound too convincing.

"What happened to your leg?" My pants were ripped away by what had been twelve-gauge shotgun blasts, and blood was dripping from my pants leg, forming a red stain on the dark asphalt.

"Just scraped it, nothing serious." Inside I knew it was futile, but it was a game you played through to the end.

"Look what I found!" A blue-uniformed officer was holding the 32 automatic carefully between two fingers.

Son-of-a-bitch! I'd stuck that damn pistol under the seat. "I never saw it before. You must have planted it." Anger at my stupidity caused me to nearly scream.

"Me neither!" Ed growled.

"You guys are both on parole. That's a felony. Hell, Gordy, I thought you were smarter than that." The detective shook his head.

Shortly after I was returned to jail, my wife, Janie, confirmed something that we had hoped for. She was pregnant. I thought that I had experienced hurt and anguish in my life, but nothing could compare with what I felt as I lay in those steel cages of the county jail. There were times when the pain and remorse became so intense I felt like banging my head against the steel bars.

My anger turned on my partner Ed, and I cursed his inability to drive a stick-shift automobile. I'd never have been in this stinking mess if that son-of-a-bitch could drive. Why the hell didn't he tell me he couldn't. The conscious decision to commit a crime was forgotten and I fixed the blame on Ed, a poor bastard who had been out of prison only four days!

Six weeks later, after the usual threats and negotiations by lawyers and prosecutors, it was decided that justice would best be served by returning us to prison as parole violators. Our screams of innocence and outrage at being discriminated against (a new defense of the sixties for ex-cons) fell on unsympathetic ears. It was a bus ride to Walla Walla and back to the "big yard."

The dramatic changes in the prison culture made doing time more difficult. But the thought of my wife and daughters out there by themselves was a hurt that was more intense than anything I'd ever experienced. I had to get out.

He was a good fighter, and he fought.

Gordon Graham:
Through the years . . .

Monroe Reformatory, where it all began. From this view, it looks well kept and tranquil.

But, from the inside, it could be this . . .

Or this — Vocational Building at Monroe after the riot.

Home?

The skin search: humiliation
that cannot be described

A.K.O. in the second round.

Golden Gloves Champs:
"The discipline to win."

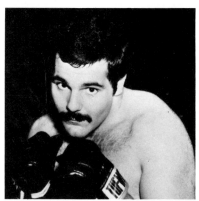

Tony Gallo.

Ed Bytheway,
just out of prison,
winning a
10-round decision.

Six months
later he died of an
overdose of heroin
at 35 years old.

Front doors to Monroe Reformatory: few people enter them by choice.

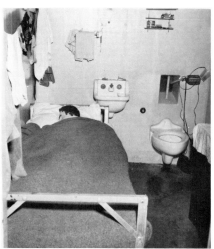

Dummies look just like people in
prison: one way to beat the count
system.

Bob Rhay, warden at
Walla Walla — a tough job.

Revisiting the Cataldo Mission. It was a refuge for two cold, hungry escapees.

Lou and Diane Tice, founders of The Pacific Institute

Fred Forsberg and Ron Medbed, at an Awareness Club

Speaking to the Walla Walla Awareness Club.

Speaking at the prison Chapel at McNeil Island Penitentiary.

Teaching a seminar to business professionals.

The happiness of marriage: Gordon and Janie.

The Graham Family, 1975.

14. Birth of a Baby

From my cell in the minimum security building, I could look across the green fields and see the area of the city where Janie lived. The urge to escape was always there, but I knew it was futile. I'd lose any chance I had of being with Janie and the girls. The thought of planting a dummy in my bed and slipping away for a few hours kept running through my mind. I knew guys who'd done it and no one had ever known they had been gone. The fear of getting caught kept me from taking the risk.

Some inmate crews from the minimum security building were allowed to work in town. The workmen were supervised by crew bosses. If you got lucky and drew a good one, you might get a chance to spend a few minutes with your wife.

The desire to see Janie and the girls was strong. I knew how much she needed me and I ached to be with her. It took every ounce of will power I had to keep from violating the trust that Bob had placed in me. I wanted out.

Janie was getting closer to her due date. When I touched her, I could feel the baby kick inside the swollen belly. My heart ached with love and a feeling of helplessness. My world revolved around visiting days and phone calls. I wanted to be there for her, not just on visiting days or at the end of a phone.

From the third floor of the minimum security building, I could see the interstate highway and the streets of Walla Walla. On visiting day I'd stand at a window on the top floor of the building and watch for Janie's red Chevy convertible. She always drove the same route and always at top speed. I'd see the dust billowing, and I knew who it was before I could ever make out the car. I watched the Chevy until it turned up the tree-covered road that led to the prison. When she was out of sight, I'd hurry down to the visiting room to wait for her.

The visiting rooms are always full of hurting people, unable to free themselves from the mental traps in which they have become entangled. There are men caught up in the fantasy life of prisons, living to get out so they can return to drugs and stealing. There are men who want to straighten their lives out and become law-abiding citizens, but are trapped by time and circumstances. There are women whose lives are tied to men through love, fear or desperation, parents unable to reach the son who has become a drug addict or a thief. There are friends reaching out, one more time, in hopes that their faith will inspire a change. The old cliche' that "misery loves company" seems so true in prisons. All of these people mingle together in one room, each with his or her own reason for being there, each caught up in his or her own world.

The visiting room fills and the fumbling hands and passionate kisses intensify. Men starved for a woman try desperately to find some way to make love, unobserved, in a straight-backed chair. Occasionally an embarrassed officer warns an over-zealous lover to remove his hands from under the lady's blouse.

Kids run wildly through the crowded visiting room, their faces hungry for love and attention, oblivious to the realities around them.

Janie and I would try to lock out the noise and the hurt. We'd spend hours talking about the future. The excitement of the baby that was now two weeks overdue filled our hearts. Tami and Tina had grown familiar with the minimum security building and most of the inmates knew them. They'd spend their time between the swings in the prison yard, the pop machine, and my lap.

When the visit ended, I'd walk Janie and the girls to the car, desperately trying to avoid the painful good-bys. "I'll call you later tonight. You be careful and call the doctor if you feel pains or anything." I longed to go with her, to hold her in my arms without fifty hurting people as an audience.

The red convertible pulled away, picking up speed. Don't speed, honey, I thought. I worry when you drive too fast. The guards had talked to me about Janie's speeding. I tried mentally to get her to slow down. I didn't care too much about the guards' complaints, but I sure as hell cared about my family's safety.

On June 11, 1971, I made my usual early morning call to Janie. She said the pains had started about 6:00 a.m. I knew in my heart today would be the day the baby would be born. I wanted to be with her. Without my knowledge, Janie had called B. J. Rhay and explained the situation to him. Because it was Friday and not a normal visiting day, a special two-hour visit was granted. Janie's doctor had decided to induce labor on Saturday the 12th. By then she would be four weeks overdue, and he felt it would be harmful to her and the baby if she went any longer.

I didn't expect to see her until after the baby was born, but I saw the red Chevy pull into the parking lot. I was afraid something was wrong. I hurried out to meet her. She told me it was time for the birth of our child.

We went into the visiting room. It was quiet; we were the only people visiting today. Janie's pains had quit. Was this a false alarm? I thought, boy I hope not. I knew she was getting tired of being pregnant. I leaned over and placed my hand gently on her belly. Janie moved it around, then pushed down.

"Feel the baby?" she said. I could feel the movement inside her, I was afraid to change position for fear it would stop.

"It's kicking like hell, baby. I think it's time to make an appearance," I said.

My mind returned to a day in October. I had just been busted and put into the system again. It was visiting day at King County Jail. Visits were structured around days of the week and the first letter of your name—for E, F, G, and H, visiting day was Monday. Janie arrived at 7:00. We had twenty minutes to visit. She looked small and fragile. But if she had any fears, they were hidden behind the beautiful smile. She now had to make plans to relocate the girls and herself. I knew it would be tough, but she showed strength I never knew she had.

We had been trying to have a baby for the past year. Every month when her period would begin, we'd try to hide the disappointment. As usual, I came up with the question I had asked so many times before. "Did you start your period, baby?"

"Start what?" Her mind was so far from my thought, she was surprised by the question.

"Your period," I said. I would lie in my cell thinking about it. You think too much in jail. Your mind is consumed with worry.

"Oh, my God no!" she replied. "I hadn't even thought about it. It was due two weeks ago." Excitement filled my heart. I could see the surprise and happiness come over her. But deep in my heart I felt I had let her down again. I should be with her and not in this jail. She needs me now more than ever, I thought.

"Visiting time is over." The guard's voice brought my mind back to Walla Walla. Our visit seemed much shorter than two hours. It was time for Janie to go. She hadn't had one labor pain while we visited, but kept assuring me the baby was going to be born before the end of the day. I guess mothers have a way of sensing that.

At 11:49 that night my wife gave birth to a seven pound baby boy. The guard in the rotunda called me to give me the news. A boy. I'd wanted it to be a boy but was afraid to wish too hard for one.

"I don't know if the state is ready for another 'Gordy Graham,' " the guard laughed.

I woke up all my partners to share the good news. "Man, am I glad to hear that. Now I can call my old lady," Ed laughed. The laughing and congratulations made me feel good.

I'd been given permission to visit Janie in the hospital. I had to have a prison guard accompany me. I asked a friend, Tony Pugliese, one of the recreational staff, if he'd take me, and he agreed to. We arrived at the hospital and they directed us to the maternity ward.

Janie looked pale and tired, but her eyes were full of love. "How you feelin', sweetheart?" I kissed her gently on the cheek and held her hand tightly against my heart.

"I feel wonderful. We've got a baby boy, Gordy. His name is Gordon Earl Graham. Do you want to see him?"

"Can we see him now? Can you walk and stuff?"

"Yes, but we've got to go kind of slow." Janie took my hand and led me out of the ward and down the hall.

"I'll wait outside for you, Gordy," the guard said.

"Come and see the baby first," I urged. He was a good guy and I liked him.

There were six or seven babies all lined up in their little cribs. There was no way to tell which one was Gordy. "Which one is he?" I turned to Janie.

"That's him, the second one from the right." He was red and wrinkled and his mouth was wide open; he was screaming like hell!

"He don't look too happy about being here."

The guard left us alone. Janie put her arms around me. "He's our baby, honey." I held her, afraid to squeeze her for fear I would hurt her. The guard was back, tapping on my shoulder. I didn't realize we'd been standing there so long.

"We're going to have to get back, Gordy." I'd forgotten about him and the joint for a minute.

"Okay, man, let me take Janie back to the ward." We walked slowly back to her room. I helped her get settled and kissed her goodby. "I'll call tonight, honey. Take care of yourself. The baby is beautiful." We walked out of the hospital. I'm always going back to prison, I thought. There's got to be an end to this kind of life! All too soon we were back behind the Walls. I felt empty—I had left a part of me behind and I wanted to have it back.

As the days passed, I tried to think of ways to be with Janie. One day Ed came in excitedly. "They passed the furlough bill, man. Shit, you ought to be able to get one. Hell, your wife just had a baby."

There had been a bill in the legislature allowing inmates nearing the end of their prison sentences a furlough to go home. The furloughs could be as long as ten days. The intent of the bill was to help inmates and families re-establish their ties. The time could also be used to look for employment. Ed continued, "My counselor said it was signed by the governor and would start right away. They've got forms you fill out, man. You oughta check it out."

"Thanks, man. I'll see my counselor and put in a request."

I contacted my counselor. After going through the appropriate amount of red tape and an intense orientation on responsibility, I was granted a furlough. I was the first inmate in the state to be allowed out on a furlough. The days dragged by and I thought Saturday would never come.

Finally, Saturday morning arrived. I was up at 5:00 a.m. Janie would pick me up at 11:30. I'd never seen Janie's home. She'd told me that it was small and sat on the edge of an onion field. I tried to picture what it would be like.

The red convertible pulled into the institution parking lot. Janie signed a paper that placed me in her charge. As we left the administration building, a prison counselor gave me last minute warnings about returning late.

Shivers ran through my body as we drove down the tree-covered lane away from the institution. I could see the tower guards, rifles in the crooks of their arms, watching as we drove away. My back felt naked in the warm noonday sun.

As soon as we were off the prison grounds, I pulled Janie into my arms. She eased the car onto the edge of the street and we held each other. No words were necessary. I could feel the wetness of tears on her cheeks and my heart swelled with emotion. "I love you, baby. It's so good to hold you. Let's go home!"

We pulled into the yard. The house was small, like a cabin. A huge maple with a tire swing hanging from a gnarled limb filled the front yard. Full sacks of freshly harvested onions were scattered across a large field at the back of the house. "You weren't kidding about the onion field!" We laughed.

I had Tina and Gordy in my arms. Janie had her arm around my waist. Tami had run ahead to hold the screen door open for us. We entered the front room. It was small, but neatly arranged, and it felt like home. I put Gordy in his crib. He was so small. Tina had gotten into a conversation with the cat and Tami was already in the swing, wanting me to push her. I looked at Janie. She was beautiful. Her eyes sparkled with pride. I couldn't remember when I had felt as good as I did at that moment.

Later, Janie was asleep. The light of the moon shone through the window, splashing a yellow-gold across her face. A warm summer breeze brought the pungent smell of onions into the bedroom. The house was loosely constructed. The wind carried the odor of onions as it seeped through the cracks and crevices in the walls. My first night home I cried all night. They picked a hell of a time to harvest their onions.

We had finished breakfast and both of us were avoiding the subject of time. Twenty-four hours goes by so fast. "We'll need to leave here about 11:45, honey. I don't want to be late." Boy, I never thought I'd return to prison by myself.

"You get to come home every week, honey. It will all end before too long." Janie's voice soothed my nerves.

Tami, Tina and Gordy were so young and so totally trusting. Tami was old enough to know that I was in prison. I'd told her that I'd done some bad things and that I had to pay for it. Tina was only two years old and really didn't understand what was going on. And now, we had "the dude," Gordy. There was no way I could let these little people down. I loved them and I felt a deep sense of commitment to making a good life for them. I had to change my life somehow.

"Well, honey, guess we'd better go." It was 11:40 and I had twenty minutes to get back to prison! We gathered up our three children and climbed into the car. My stomach churned and I had to force myself not to think about going back. I had all three of the kids in my lap when we pulled into the prison parking lot. It was 11:53. We'd made it in thirteen minutes. This time, I wasn't "on" Janie about her fast driving!

Janie and I checked into the rotunda and the guard signed me in. "I'll call you later tonight, honey. See you on visiting day."

"Let's go, Gordy. We've got to shake you down." The guard had the gate open, waiting. I was a prisoner again. I watched Janie walk away, her arms full of kids. She had become the central point in my life. Her love and belief were causing me to make decisions I'd never made before. Meeting her was the best thing that had ever happened to me.

The furloughs continued each week. I kept expecting them to end. It was too good to be true. There were men being allowed to leave the institution to speak at schools and social clubs. Now work release was in full swing. It was an era of freedom and responsibility. I became caught up in the frantic pace of the late sixties.

15. A Job?

It was during this time of social change that I first met Greg Barlow. We were in the visiting room of the Washington State Penitentiary. One of the three visitors from Olympia was speaking. "We're from the State Board of Community Colleges, and we have been asked to do a study of the educational and vocational opportunities in the four adult correctional institutions in the state. I'm Greg Barlow, Director of Special Projects, and this is Susan Nelle." He turned to a dark-haired woman with a pretty face. Her eyes sparkled with excitement and warmth. He introduced the third member of the group as Allen Suver. "What we would like from you is some of your feelings about the educational and vocational programs. Are they relevant? How many people can they accommodate? Are the instructors qualified? Anything you feel would help in the programs' success. We want your input."

There were four inmates including myself who had been selected to represent the twelve hundred men inside the walls of the penitentiary. They all looked to me for direction. We were members of the inmate government, elected by the population to represent them with the administration and to negotiate for better conditions within the Walls.

I looked at my partners. Ed was leaning back in his chair. He had been doing time with me for fifteen years. Ed had tremendous talent as an athlete, but drugs and penitentiaries had eaten away most of the goodness. He had become a dangerous individual. Most of the inmates and staff were afraid of him.

John was a bank robber, sophisticated as a convict, but shallow as a man. He hadn't done much time, but he was an apparent survivor. He was the kind of person you knew would break under pressure or fear. You had to be careful about what he knew.

The fourth member of our group was a slender black called "Slick." He was the vice president of the inmate government. Slick was a good guy with a great sense of humor. If you could keep him straight, he was capable of displaying excellent leadership ability. Between the two of us, we could settle most of the racial conflicts that developed inside the penitentiary. He had a real weakness for drugs and had a tendency to go on the "nod" at the most inappropriate times.

Earlier in the year, we had been in a crucial meeting with the State Parole Board. We were trying to convince them of the importance of inmate input into institutional management. Slick was loaded on "yellow jackets" (a sleeping pill). He suddenly fell out of his chair and landed on the floor where he lay quietly. He lay there motionless, a silly grin spread across his face. Needless to say, we weren't too convincing after that.

My thoughts focused on the futility of another study.

Both Ed and Slick were hung up on the dark-haired lady, who seemed unaware of the impact her smile was having on them. John was busy taking notes and asking the one called Greg questions filled with all kinds of impressive words. "Are you looking at an empirical study, and if so, how do you plan on identifying a control group?" He poised his pen for the answer.

"What the fuck is he talking about?" Slick whispered.

I interrupted John's fascination with the sound of his own voice. "Let me tell you how we feel about studies. They've been conducting studies in here for as long as I've been doing time, and that's damn near forever. The studies all came up with the same conclusions, but nothing ever happens. All sorts of people who don't know a damn thing about life in a joint parade in and out of here. They get a federal grant to study something, and right now convicts are a fad, so they come in here and use us as guinea pigs. The people in here are tired of being studied. If you've got some of those federal dollars, just split 'em up and give 'em to the first ten guys who leave this joint and the money will do a hell of a lot more good!''

The lady's smile was gone and the two college professors looked like they'd been hit with a bucket of ice water. Slick was awake now. "He's telling you right, man. The dudes in here are really up tight about people coming in here acting like they're in a zoo staring at monkeys."

Ed was still hung up on the lady, but I knew he would support any move we made. John looked hurt. We'd messed up his opportunity to impress these people with his intelligence. I looked at my three partners, then back at the people on the committee.

Greg looked right at me. His eyes didn't shift when they locked with mine. "I appreciate your honesty and can understand how you feel. We really don't know anything about prisons, but if we do the right kind of study, we can present our findings to the legislative body and possibly open up some new opportunities for you people. But the only way the study can tell the real story is if we can get the inmates to be honest and to cooperate with us. That's why we wanted to meet with you first. You can give us the information we need." He stopped and turned to the young woman.

"Ms. Nelle is a clinical psychologist. Her expertise is in research and writing. Alan is the Dean of Education at Bellevue Community College. We have the kind of people supporting this effort who can have a real impact. We also have an ex-convict who is involved on the study team. You probably know him, David Grant. He works for me at the State Board.

I knew Dave. We'd done a lot of time together. He had been my tight end on the "Stealers" football team. "Yeah, Dave's a good guy. How's he doing?" I remembered Dave as a guy who'd had a lot of challenges with booze.

"He's doing okay. He goes on an extended canoe trip once in a while, but he's a good guy." I knew the extended canoe trips had something to do with his alcohol challenge.

Ed took his eyes off Susan. "Hey, man, you ought to hire me. I could really give your study credibility."

Slick laughed, "Hell, man, you're doing five years. I'm short. They need some color on their study team!"

John took his shot. "I worked on a study in California with the Youth Authority, and when I was at Cal Poly, I was into a lot of research." Boy, if they go for that, they'll go for fried ice cream, I thought.

My mind was suddenly in a race. There's got to be a way to use this situation to get out of this joint! Every day had become a battle for survival.

As I looked around the visiting room at the naive middle-class college professors, a feeling of resentment came over me. "I don't want to sound hostile, but there's some things that you have to hear about penitentiaries and the people that live here. The day before yesterday at breakfast, an inmate who wasn't playing with a full deck accidentally bumped into a dude in the mess hall and spilled the guy's cup of milk. The guy pulled a shank and stabbed the poor senseless bastard about ten times before anyone could stop him! Last week a guy got thrown off the third tier in eight-wing 'cause somebody didn't want him in the cell anymore! There's been at least ten armed robberies on the breezeway in the last two weeks! 'Big Red' (the isolation unit) is full of guys who are locked up for their own protection. Not because they've done anything, but because they're afraid!"

"Now, let me ask you a question. How can you talk about educational or vocational training without considering the totality of the situation? How can anyone get involved in education if he's consumed with survival? You can't conduct a study without taking these things into consideration. You can't isolate one aspect of an institution. Each part has an impact on the other!"

My voice shook with emotion and the intensity of my words had caused tears to well up in my eyes. They don't understand what the hell I'm talking about, I thought. Shit, it's insane. "You seem like a sincere group of people. We'll cooperate and we'll ask the cons to talk openly to you. Hell, I guess another study won't kill anyone, but don't expect a lot to happen. How do you guys feel about it?" I turned to my partners. Slick nodded his head in agreement.

Ed looked at Susan and said, "I'll make sure no one bothers you. If you need anything, ask for Ed Bytheway."

John folded his papers and, trying to sound official, said, "I'll start putting together some figures for you on how many people are enrolled in school and send them to you."

We shook hands. Ed walked over and gripped the bars of the steel door that had been locked by the guard in the room outside. "Key up!" he called.

Greg, the director, tapped me on the shoulder and said, "Can we talk a minute in private?"

I turned to John. "I'll be right with you. Wait for me outside." Greg and I walked over to the corner of the visiting room.

"I'm interested in what you had to say. Those are things we need to be aware of. How much time do you have to do?"

"I'm doing five years on a parole violation. I've only got a year or so in, but I figure to get a release date when I go to the parole board next month."

"We've got a position open on the study team and I'd like to see if we could get you out on work release. Would you be interested?"

Excitement filled me. I tried to appear calm. "Sure, I think I could offer something to your group, and I think B. J., the warden, would approve me for work release." Wait till I call Janie! I was anxious to get to a phone and let her in on the good news.

Two months later I was transferred to a work release facility in Tacoma. The job with the State Board had become a reality. I was a member of the study team. But what the hell was I to do next?

16. Federal Gravy Train

My world changed rapidly in those early months. My experience with the State Board of Community Colleges gave me confidence and established a small network of friends from that "other world." My background had become an asset. Seventeen years in prison, convict leader, all these heretofore negative factors suddenly were seen as valuable.

Greg Barlow, my initial contact and benefactor, lent support and encouragement. He was younger than I in years, but older in wisdom of this "new world." He was a helicopter pilot and a decorated Viet Nam veteran. There was a strong spiritual belief that shone through his professional armor. He had tremendous faith in me and provided opportunities that caused me to grow rapidly in many areas.

Susan Nelle, Greg's assistant, was a woman who exhibited love and a desire to make the world a better place in the midst of an era of violence and revolution. Her goodness and skill in writing provided support and guidance and helped develop the potential that lay dormant inside me those many years behind bars.

Lieta, a beautiful Philippine lady, twenty-one years old, reached out her hand to me. She was a secretary with great energy and a desire to be something more. In the alien world of college professors, she brought a breath of honesty and light that enriched my life.

There were others who befriended me during that period of my life, and there were those who resented me. All contributed to my development, and in their own ways, all contributed to who I am today.

The first months out of prison, I kept wondering how long I could last. Here I was, a five-time loser, trying to find myself a niche in the world of law-abiding citizens. Few people gave me much of a chance. The majority seemed to feel that it was just a matter of time before I stumbled and fell. They were convinced there was no way I could be doing right.

The fear of being set up or framed was constantly on my mind. Many felt anger at the thought of me driving a state car or collecting a pay check from the State Board of Community Colleges. Letters were sent to law enforcement agencies and to the governor, warning them about my danger to society. Rumors about my being involved in robberies, drugs and any other crimes being committed spread throughout the state. The pressures were tremendous and I wondered if it was worth all the effort.

When I traveled across the state, I would have service station attendants sign their names and the time I was there on my gas receipts. If I stopped at restaurants, I requested the waitresses' signatures on my checks. I documented my whereabouts at all times. These precautions gave me some comfort in the event I were mistakenly accused of a crime.

When I visited Monroe or Walla Walla, I could feel the hostility of many prison officials and the outrage of prison guards. I tried not to add any fuel to the fire. My manners were polite and I exhibited as much humility as possible. These people had known me for twenty years as a convict, a manipulator and a thief. It would take years for their attitudes to change.

The five-hundred-and-twenty-dollar-a-month salary had been the first money I'd received from a legal effort. It had been tough for Janie and the children. We had moved into a duplex in Lacey, a small city near the state capitol, Olympia. Janie had gotten a part-time job in the evenings with a janitorial service, and between our two salaries, we managed to survive without my stealing.

It had been four months since I'd been released from the Walls. I still felt isolated and out of place in this office full of educators. The prison study had been completed and the final draft was at the printers. We really hadn't learned anything new. The findings revealed that there were not enough opportunities in the vocational trades; they also suggested that many of the skills being taught were not applicable in the real world. This had been common knowledge among staff and inmates for years. Seventy thousand dollars for something that any prison official or inmate could have told them. But I wasn't complaining; the study had gotten me out of prison.

I hadn't learned anything new about prisons. However, I had learned a great deal about how the system worked. Federal dollars were being pumped into the states to help misguided convicts. It seemed like everywhere I went there were ex-cons running programs, driving state cars . . . hell, there were even four or five who were parole officers. This couldn't go on; all this federal money had to dry up.

My position at the State Board was about to be terminated. Greg and I were exploring ways for me to continue with the board in some new capacity. I needed to come up with a way to continue my work, to stay on the outside.

I decided that what the system really needed was someone who would set up and coordinate the educational and vocational opportunities for the convicts in the twenty-eight community colleges in the state. It really didn't matter that there wasn't much to coordinate. Hell, a system that would spend $70,000 just to study the opportunities should really get excited about coordination! I approached Greg with my idea. He said it sounded good to him, so I wrote up a job description that fit my unique qualifications and established a salary that seemed consistent with what Greg thought was being paid for similar positions.

To my amazement, the position was accepted, and I became the first Correctional Education Coordinator for the State Board of Community Colleges. I'd begun to think that just maybe I could plug into this ''monster'' called society.

I was driving around the state in an official government car, visiting the prisons, trying to figure out how the hell to make something happen that would benefit the convicts. Correctional staff who knew me were either openly hostile or skeptical of my intent. Convicts who knew me gave me credit for running a smooth game on the Man.

It was easier to be honest than dishonest, so I just leaned back and enjoyed being involved in this strange society, even though I knew I didn't belong! At home in our duplex I would wrap myself up in the warmth of our family, loving and being loved. But morning would come or the weekend would swiftly disappear and I would have to go back out and face that alien world.

Much of my time was spent thinking about stealing and ways to rip off the system. Many of my former partners would send word on their activities and ask me to join them. Janie and our three kids gave me strength to say "no." I was beginning to let go of the idea of ripping someone off for the sake of getting even, and it felt good.

It was a time when the convict employee, especially the one who was articulate and had learned to manipulate the system, was perceived by many employers as an excellent addition to their staffs. The company or government agency that hired the ex-convict was given certain status. It was a time when the "you've got to be one to relate to one" idea became an accepted theory. The ex-convicts who entered these employment positions were protected from many of the accepted standards of a productive work environment. Tardiness, for example, was excused as an adjustment problem.

The federal government, caught in the wave of social conscience, responded by pouring money into programs for the disadvantaged. A myriad of non-profit agencies sprang up, funded by federal dollars. Ex-convicts were made eligible for millions of federal dollars to be utilized to help in their reintegration. Grant writers were at a premium and empirical data, peer counseling and half-way house became common terminology. National conferences, workshops and seminars centered around prisons. Travel by air to national conferences became routine for people who had never traveled outside of their hometowns. Conferences on convicts' rights, prisons, sensitivity and human relations were attended by thousands of people, all on the government ticket. Role playing became an "in thing." Parole officers and correctional staff were asked to simulate the life style of a convict or thief. Workshop leaders, speakers, and other consultants were sought out as drawing cards. Large honorariums, first class travel and expenses were available, all on Uncle Sam.

My background in prison as a convict leader and my ability to talk fluently to others about prison and prisoners began to attract attention. People running workshops and conferences began seeking me out. I began to travel to other parts of the country as a speaker: Colorado, Minnesota, and California. I began to understand the game of using the convict as a vehicle to attain federal dollars. My ability to communicate and the feeling of personal achievement I gained from these opportunities began to change my perception. I began to realize that I could contribute something to society, that perhaps I could become part of this world.

My knowledge of prisons increased. At meetings or social gatherings, I could participate in conversations as long as they centered around prisons or the criminal justice system. If the conversation drifted to other topics, I became quiet and withdrawn. I had no awareness of social issues and politics. Taxes made no sense to me. The prime rate had to do with beef steak; my only value was my time in prison.

I began to feel like the "pet convict," paid to perform, to talk of life in prison, to be humble, to continually express my gratitude and appreciation to my benefactors. I was constantly reminded, ever so subtly, just how much I owed them.

However, the positive environment, the loose-knit support group, the accumulative wins began to have an impact on my attitude and my behavior. The unconditional love of my wife and three children, the responsibilities of being a father and husband: these factors gradually began to change my picture of reality.

For many, ex-con and private citizen alike, the same set of circumstances that changed my life became a way to rip off the system.

Paper programs full of statistics and success stories were fronts for large salaries and self-serving corporations. Non-profit agencies were used to funnel federal dollars into profit-making ventures. The convict and the purpose of the federal dollars became lost in greed and dishonesty. For every person whose life changed during this period (and I know of many), thousands of others were misled, deceived and became more firmly entrenched in a life of crime.

I'd had an opportunity to participate in one or two educational seminars sponsored by the State Board. There always seemed to be a workshop or seminar being promoted at the urging of friends. Janie and I allowed ourselves to be scheduled into a week-end program called an "image seminar."

17. The Pacific Institute

Port Ludlow, a resort and conference center that sits on the Hood Canal about forty miles and a thirty minute ferry ride from Seattle, was to be the site of the Image Seminar. Janie and I had never been to anything like this before, and I was nervous. Hell, I'd only been out of prison a few months and was having enough trouble adjusting to my job with the State Board. Now I had to deal with this damn seminar. Why the hell did I let those guys talk me into going to this thing! The closer we got to Port Ludlow, the more nervous I became.

Wally and Joe were friends I'd met through a mutual interest in professional boxing. Joe was a local fight promoter and Wally sold Cadillacs. I'd been hanging around them with the idea of picking up a few extra dollars by getting a fight or two. I was a little old, but you can always get a fight if you are in condition and have a little style, and I needed the money. We'd met in the gym one day, and they were both excited about an Image Seminar they'd attended. They were convinced it was something I'd enjoy and be able to use. I wasn't interested in seminars and told them that I was more interested in getting on a fight card scheduled for Seattle.

When they'd failed to sell me on the value of the Image Seminar, they decided I should meet with Lou Tice, the man who would lead the seminar, and have him explain how it might help me. Finally I agreed to meet this guy they were so excited about.

We met a few days later at a waterfront restaurant in Seattle. Lou Tice was already there when Wally, Joe and I arrived. He was sitting at a table for four overlooking the water. The waiter led us to his table, and Joe introduced us. Lou stood up. He was shorter than I had imagined based on Wally's and Joe's description. I had expected someone 6′6′′ with a Charles Atlas build. He was about 5′8′′ and slightly overweight, with a round face and light brown hair. His handshake was firm and his voice was strong and confident.

"These two have spoken highly of you and what you're doing. It's a pleasure to meet you." His voice was sincere and right off I liked him.

"That's nice of them. They've told me about your seminars and your plans to start a 'girls town.' It sure is needed. There aren't many options for young women in the state."

The waiter was standing over us and Wally and Joe ordered dinner. I was uncomfortable now and didn't really know what to order, so I just said, "Let me have the same."

We talked for a while about the weather and how the football teams were doing. I discovered that Lou had recently left his job as head football coach and athletic director of a Catholic high school. He'd developed a powerful team using the principles taught in his seminars. This caused me to listen a little more closely. I'd always been involved in athletics in prison and had been a pro-fighter. I could relate to sports. He talked about mental barriers that keep athletes from achieving and how these barriers relate to the people's self-image or what they believe to be the truth about themselves. His seminars were designed to help people recognize these barriers and change their self-images. A young man who knew he couldn't bench press 220 pounds kept failing, but after changing his self-image, he was able to lift 240.

Lou also talked about Comfort Zones. He said that we develop a Comfort Zone that corresponds with our self-image, and that when we get out of our Comfort Zone, we get up tight.

"Our first tendency will be to get back where we belong; if we can't, then we will recreate our Comfort Zone wherever we are. It's my feeling that prison can be a Comfort Zone and that when people get out, they are unable to adjust and end up doing something to get back. What's your feeling on this?''

My mind was racing. I thought of all the times I'd gotten out of prison and felt out of place. The times that I'd done something stupid and had been returned to prison. How I'd surrounded myself with ex-cons when I was on the street.

"It sure makes sense to me. I can really see how prisons can be a Comfort Zone. They need to get this kind of information to guys in prison.''

Joe and Wally looked at each other with satisfied grins. But I was too intent on what I'd heard and what Lou was saying to let their smugness bother me.

Lou continued, "Wally seems to think that you have the ability to help improve the corrections system of America. I want to fund a girls' town; maybe we can help each other. We've got a seminar scheduled at the end of the month. I'd like to have you and your wife attend as my guests.''

"I'd like to, but we've got three kids and we'll need to find a babysitter, and Joe and Wally said you start Thursday night, so I'd need to get off work on Friday.''

"Don't think of all the reasons why you can't. Just decide you want to and you'll come up with a way,'' he said.

"Well, I know Greg will let me off on Friday, and I think I know someone who'll watch the kids.'' It seemed easier just thinking about it now.

"We're both going back this month so we can all be there together.'' Joe spoke and I realized that I'd been so involved in what Lou was saying I'd almost forgotten about him and Wally.

"We must be getting close, honey.'' Janie's voice startled me. I'd been lost in thought.

"I don't like this, baby. Maybe we ought to pass on the seminar.''

I was beginning to consider turning the Chevy around when we topped a small rise and the resort came into view. It was a beautiful sight. The late August sun was just beginning to drop behind the hills, casting cool shadows over the neatly manicured lawn. The sloping hillside seemed to edge its way into the green waters of the canal.

A marina was lined with boats of all sizes and shapes. The main road wound down the hillside to the club house and registration office. Streets named after trees led to rows of expensive-looking condominiums.

"This is beautiful." Janie's voice sounded excited.

"Must cost a fortune to stay here. I'm sure glad they're picking up our expenses."

We drove up to the club house. The old red Chevy convertible seemed as out of place as I felt. The parking lot was about half full. Most of the cars were Cadillacs, Mercedes and Lincolns.

"Look at those cars. What the hell are we doing here, baby? Christ, I feel like getting out of here."

"Let's give it a chance, honey. We don't have anything to lose." Janie sounded confident, and her eyes were bright with excitement.

"I love you, lady!" She leaned against me, and I put my arm around her shoulder and pulled her closer as we walked to the club house. There was a restaurant with high beamed ceilings on the top floor. It had huge plate glass windows that overlooked the marina. The water of the canal was alive with color as sailboats slid across the blue surface. Mountains lay in the distance, the sun painting them beautiful shades of orange and green as it slowly sank in the west.

The scene was breathtaking; my thoughts suddenly shifted to the drab yellow bowels of six-wing at the state penitentiary. Poor bastards—wonder what they're doing right now.

"Let's get registered and find out where we're staying." Janie's voice brought me back to Port Ludlow. We went over to the registration desk. A middle-aged woman with a friendly smile came over.

"Can I help you?"

"Yes, we should have reservations. Gordon and Jane Graham?"

I watched her thumb through a stack of cards.

C'mon, lady, we must have reservations, I urged silently.

Finally she asked, "Are you with a group?"

"Yes, we're going to a seminar by Lou Tice from The Pacific Institute," Janie answered.

The lady reached over and picked up a clipboard and ran her finger down a list of names.

"Yes, here you are. Just fill out the registration form. Mr. Tice has requested that your room be included on his charges."

I was relieved. Joe and Wally had said my room would be taken care of, but I didn't know how. I knew that we couldn't afford to stay in a place like Port Ludlow on my salary. We finished filling out the form and the lady handed us two keys. "You're staying here." She pointed to a map on the desk. "Just go back up the hill to Elms. You're in the third condominium. Enjoy your stay and if you need anything, just call the desk."

We walked back to our car. The evening breeze was coming off the canal and the light scent of pines and salt water gave it a warm freshness. I breathed deeply.

"It's a beautiful place."

Our condo was situated on the hillside with a full view of the canal. Somehow every building seemed to be facing the water with the same spectacular view.

"Let's go in and see what it's like and then I'll get our things." We walked up a short flight of stairs, Janie unlocked the door and we entered. The room had a high open-beamed ceiling, a fireplace, and sliding glass doors that led out to the patio overlooking the water.

"Boy, this is great. What a neat place." Janie was standing in the middle of the room, looking out at the water in the distance. I walked over and put my arm around her.

"You like it, baby? Can you imagine what a place like this would cost? It sure is nice of Lou to pick up the tab."

The phone was ringing in our condominium. I was jerked sharply back to reality. It was Joe calling to invite us to meet them in the lounge.

"We can all go up to the conference center together."

"Sounds great—let me check with Janie."

"You want to meet Joe and Wally and their wives for a cocktail before we go to the seminar?" She nodded yes. I told Joe we'd meet them in about thirty minutes.

"I'll never go back to prison, honey." The words sounded strange and out of place in the peace and tranquility of the condominium.

"I know that, Gordy." She took my hand; I felt a deep sense of loneliness and fear for a moment and then it was gone.

"You ready, Janie?" She looked so young and beautiful. She'd spent a great deal of time preparing and I knew she was nervous about the seminar. I put my arms around her. "You look super, lady. I'm a lucky man."

We met the others in the lounge. They were all excited about being able to share the seminar with us. I felt a lot better now that we weren't going into the conference center by ourselves.

"How many people will be at the session?" I tried to sound disinterested.

"There'll be sixty to sixty-five," Joe answered. "Most will be from the business world, but there's usually some coaches, athletes and teachers. It's a wide variety of people."

I squeezed Janie's hand. She pressed closer to me, and I knew she understood. It was really tough for me to be around people who were honest and successful. I'd been dishonest and a loser all of my life. Our social life had been minimal since I'd gotten out of prison six months before. We'd never been to anything like this. Janie's closeness and her ability to know instinctively how I felt gave me strength.

The conference center sat off by itself among the trees. The round, one-story wooden building seemed to blend into the landscape like a huge tree stump. The parking lot was filling with cars as we walked up the stone pathway. People were laughing and joking as they streamed through the doors.

The room was alive with activity when we entered. About half the chairs were filled with well-dressed, smiling people. The room was set up in a U-shape with a large green chalkboard in the center. The tables were decorated with bouquets of flowers. Nameplate, notebook and pen were neatly arranged at each seat. I glanced around nervously. Most of the sixty-odd people were seated at their respective tables. They all looked so sophisticated and successful. I spotted our names and took Janie's hand, and we eased our way through the room. We were seated directly in front of the chalkboard.

Lou must want to keep his eye on me, I thought.

There was a typed list of all the participants at each seat. The names, titles and businesses were listed. I picked mine up and read down the list. The president of a construction firm, the coach from a local college, a professional football player, a professor, a doctor, a sales manager, a bank president. Geez, these people are already successful—what the hell are they doing here? I came to our names: Gordon and Janie Graham, Correctional Education Coordinator for the State Board of Community Colleges. The title sounded impressive.

What the hell do we have in common with this group? Maybe we shouldn't have come.

I felt like everyone was looking at me. The guy's an ex-con, just out of prison. It was like my past was plastered on my forehead.

I should have worn a tie.

It seems like everyone else knows everybody. There's a guy without a tie. He looks like he's rich enough not to wear one.

Thoughts kept running through my mind. Six months ago you were in prison.

Damn. Three and a half days of sitting here, trying not to look at anyone.

Janie's hand brushed my leg; I reached down and squeezed it. My palms were wet with perspiration.

I noticed a coffee urn at the back of the room.

"Do you want a cup of coffee, honey?" I whispered.

"Yes, please."

Now I have to go all the way back there to get it. I stood up and had begun to ease my way through the people when I felt a hand on my shoulder and Lou said, "Gordy, how are you?" He shook my hand and walked over to Janie and kissed her lightly on the cheek.

"I'm so glad you made it." He sounded genuinely pleased to see us. I felt better. Lou was dressed in a neat three-piece suit and his manner was relaxed and confident. I envied his confidence and the easy way he moved through the room, greeting people by their names, shaking hands with the men and greeting the ladies with a light kiss on the cheek.

I'd probably bump heads and break someone's nose if I tried that, I thought.

I'd returned with our coffee just as Lou stepped to the center of the room and stopped in front of the chalkboard.

Lou began to speak. "Hello, I'm Lou Tice, president and founder of The Pacific Institute. I want to welcome all of you to the Image Seminar."

His voice wasn't loud, but it seemed to fill the room. There was a confident strength in his words that made you feel that he had something important to say. The room was totally silent. He continued to give background information on himself and The Pacific Institute.

He'd been a football coach and athletic director at a Catholic high school. He and his wife, Diane, had a number of adopted and foster children. His company was new and was in the business of education through seminars.

When he completed his introduction, he asked the participants to stand and introduce themselves.

"Please give us a brief description of your business or profession. Let's start over here on my left." He pointed to a dark-haired couple seated in the last two chairs in the row.

The man stood. He looked to be in his mid-thirties. He introduced himself as Harold Johnston, a manager at the Everett Trust and Savings Bank. His wife's name was Jan, and she was a teacher in junior high school. As the couples stood and introduced themselves, I was amazed at their positions. They all seemed at ease and had something interesting or humorous to add. It was getting close to my turn, and I was trying frantically to think of something clever to say, but my mind was a blank.

"Would you introduce yourself and your lovely wife?" Lou was looking directly at me. Why didn't I stand? Now everyone is looking at me. I felt awkward as I stood.

"I'm Gordon Graham, Correctional Education Coordinator for the State Board of Community Colleges."

I started to sit down, but Lou asked, "What does a Correctional Ed Coordinator do?"

"Well, I'm responsible for establishing educational programs for inmates who are being released from prison." It sounded out of place in this room full of professionals. I hurriedly sat back down, feeling my face flush in embarrassment. Lou was still looking at me as I sat down. The next person seemed to be waiting and I felt Janie kick me on the ankle.

Geez, I forgot to introduce Janie. I stood up again, my face red.

"This is my wife, Janie; we have three children. I forgot to introduce her." Everyone laughed as I sat down.

How the hell could I forget to introduce Janie when she was sitting right next to me?

I looked at Janie, and with my lips I mouthed, "I'm sorry, honey." She smiled and I knew she understood. She had gotten used to my lack of social skills. We had been together for about four years. Most of that time I'd been in prison and she knew how tough the adjustment had been.

When the introductions were complete, Lou began the seminar.

"This seminar is a program designed to increase personal fulfillment. We will be covering a number of psychological concepts that deal with what's right with people. Most studies have centered around what's wrong with people. The concept of Self-Image Psychology is based on the premise that each of us develops a picture that we refer to as the truth. How fast we are, how smart we are, how good we are, this picture is called a self-image. It's like we are born into this world with a blank canvas in here." He tapped his forehead. "Neither good nor bad, neither winners or losers. Then we begin to put brushstrokes on the canvas. The brushstrokes are our experiences, the information we accept from experts, and gradually we paint a picture, or develop a self-image. If we have accepted a great deal of negative information or our experiences have been negative, then we develop a faulty picture. Who have you listened to? Who are your experts?'' I thought of the convicts and prison staff who'd given me feedback, the experiences that had been my brushstrokes.

''When we move away from our self-image or try hard to different, we begin to get feedback that makes us feel out of place. It could be a new job, a new home or a change of environment. Where do you feel out of place?'' I felt as though everyone was looking at me. They must know I'm just out of prison.

Janie and I were back in our condominium. The first session of the seminar had hit me like a ton of bricks. I'd seen myself in every example Lou had used!

I was almost afraid to ask Janie what she had thought of the evening session. We were lying on the bed. You could see the reflection of the moon bouncing off the water. It was past midnight, but I was wide awake. I could feel Janie next to me, and I knew she was waiting for me to talk about the seminar.

''What did you think, honey?'' I didn't want her to know, just yet, how deeply it had affected me.

''I thought it was interesting. He's sure a good teacher. What did you think?''

''I felt like he was talking to me all night. I learned more tonight than I ever have before about who I am and why I've been in trouble all my life.'' A strange new strength and conviction had come over me. I continued, ''This kind of information needs to be in prisons. Every person should have access to these concepts.'' As I was speaking, I began to know what I wanted to do. I wanted to take these concepts to prisons and prisoners. I began getting excited. ''Janie, this information could keep people from going back to prison. Somehow I want to get this stuff back to the people I know who are behind the Walls.''

We talked for a few minutes. My mind was spinning and I knew Janie was tired. ''You better get to sleep, baby. We've got a long day tomorrow.'' She closed her eyes and I felt a deep sense of gratitude for Janie's involvement in my life.

18. Learning to See

When I returned from Port Ludlow, I spent hours reviewing my notes and writing out my goals and affirmations. My first reaction to the seminar was a feeling that I could be free, that I could become an honest person. The idea of taking control of what you think about was so basic and yet so logical. Affirmations designed to discipline your mind and your thought patterns made sense to me. Taking on accountability for your life, seeing that there were choices and that you were responsible for those choices seemed like profound wisdom. Recognizing that you can change attitudes that hold you back and that it's okay to be uncomfortable and to feel out of place and that others feel the same way brought a new awareness to me. The power of goal setting and thinking about what you want, not what you don't want, seemed amazingly simple. All of these ideas pulled together created a sense of power. It was as though a light switched on, and I knew instinctively it was over. I could see. Not clearly, but I could see.

Two days after that first seminar, I was standing outside the small art studio that served as the office for The Pacific Institute. Lou Tice was talking. "You know, Gordy, you have a doctorate that nobody would ever want to pay for. If you combine your experience with the concepts and techniques that I teach, we could change the correctional system of America." To anyone else, the idea of an ex-convict and a former football coach teaming up to change the correctional system of this country might seem absurd, but it sounded reasonable to me.

"What do I need to do?" Excitement charged through me and I wanted to start now.

"I want you to start going with me when I teach. I'll give you audio tapes and reading materials to begin study."

For the first time, I felt that I had a chance to make it in the honest world. I had a sense of purpose, a goal, and a wife and family who gave me courage. But old habits and attitudes take time to change. I still had the feeling that someday the right opportunity would present itself, and that when it did, it would be my chance to get even. Each day I had to beat back the desire to solve my financial problems through dishonest means. The temptations were everywhere. Old friends would call and invite me to join them in a burglary or take part in a robbery. An open cash drawer in a department store or a safe left open by a clerk would get through my awareness and I would hurry away, fighting the urge to take one chance.

The feelings began to subside. The temptations seemed less and less inviting. My desire to change grew stronger with each passing day. For the next few months, I immersed myself in Self-Image Psychology. I read everything I could find and my home was filled with the voice of Lou Tice. I traveled with Lou to seminars until I could anticipate every word before he would speak. Examples from my own life would come to mind and I'd jot them down. Then I began to take one concept and teach while Lou sat quietly in the audience. The new ways of thinking and behaving became more and more a part of me. I studied other teachers and other concepts. I devoured volumes of knowledge and practiced in my mind.

I was also using the concepts in my business life. My job had concluded at the community college, and I was hired to direct a program at the University of Washington. My goal was to teach seminars in prisons to effect the kinds of changes that Lou and I had talked about, but I wasn't ready yet. I needed to support myself and my family, so when the offer for the position at the university was presented to me, I eagerly accepted.

My work with inmates through the community colleges had drawn the attention of the Vice President for Minority Affairs, Sam Kelly. He had encountered endless problems developing consistent leadership for the Resident Project and felt my involvement could help resolve some of these challenges.

The Resident Release Program offered room, board and tuition for inmates who were nearing their release from prison. Those inmates who qualified were transferred from the prison to a co-educational dormitory on campus. They were under the supervision of a staff employed by the university. When inmates were not in classes, they were expected to be in the dormitory. The guidelines included twenty-four-hour supervision and a check in, check out system designed to monitor the inmates' activities.

When Sam offered me the job as director of this program at a salary of $13,500 a year, I was overwhelmed. He was a retired Army colonel and a warrior in the battle for equal opportunity. I had always had a great deal of respect for him and was genuinely flattered by his offer. Sam and I had met during my time with the State Board. An unspoken friendship and a mutual respect had begun developing from that first meeting. Sam's confidence gave me the courage to accept the position and to make it work.

This would be only my second job and I would have responsibility for a staff of eight people and supervision of thirty to forty inmates. Most of my staff members had degrees in psychology or counseling, but no experience in dealing with sophisticated convicts. It was their responsibility to supervise, counsel and offer some tutoring to the inmates within the program, and it was my responsibility to manage the project and the staff.

The late sixties and early seventies had brought about significant changes in the guidelines and the behavior expected of men and women on parole from prison. In the past, association with another ex-felon was grounds for parole revocation and return to prison. You now found men who were on active parole supervising other ex-felons. Employment for an ex-con had been a major obstacle in my earlier experience on parole. Now there were countless agencies specificially funded to secure employment for the ex-felon. Educational institutions began to realize the potential money available for convicts. Programs like the Resident Release Project were developed on campuses throughout the country. Some of these programs would fund the inmates' education all the way through a four year degree. It was a part of the federally funded "gravy train."

The university job was my first real opportunity to supervise other people. When I took over the director's post, there were approximately thirty inmates in the program. The inmates ranged from a forty-year-old who was doing a life sentence for murder to eighteen-year-olds who were doing time for car theft. They were black, white and brown. Some had long histories of doing time; others were "first timers" who really had no business being in prison. There were reformed alcoholics and former drug addicts. Drugs and alcohol presented a constant challenge. I became familiar with the controls available: antibuse for the alcoholic and urinalysis for the drug addict.

Twenty-four hours a day I was dealing with the pressures of people who had no sense of responsibility and who could rationalize any behavior to fit their particular circumstances. A few short years earlier, I had been a part of this world.

A slight error or misjudgement could become a felony. It is difficult to set up real-life situations in a controlled environment. I knew that to grow, the inmates needed opportunities to experience set-backs and to deal with conflicts. I opened the program up and increased individual responsibility. When the individuals failed to operate within the guidelines, they were expected to accept the penalty clauses outlined in the program manual.

It was my responsibility to decide whether to keep an inmate in the program or send him or her back to prison. Each time I faced a critical decision, there was a struggle between the old "convict code" and my responsibilities to Sam and the university. Each time, my loyalty to Sam and the strength of my new convictions won out. When I had to send someone back to prison, I would go home and drown my sorrows in bourbon and seek comfort from Janie's strength. I faced decisions daily that tested my commitment to my family and to those people who had placed their trust in me.

I still felt out of place in many situations and had trouble participating in conversations that didn't center around prisons or prisoners. There were seldom any thoughts of dishonesty or stealing, and I realized one day after walking out of a supermarket that I no longer noticed the make and location of the safe. The change I had felt was possible was actually happening to me.

Although I had lived most of my life as a convict and had a good understanding of the prison mentality, I had no idea how difficult it was for these people to change their behavioral patterns. Change is difficult under the best of circumstances; in an environment where pressure or anxiety is present, the process of change can be an extreme challenge. You can change knowledge, and, properly managed, you can change attitudes, but when people are under pressure or face difficult decisions, they revert to the behavior that is most familiar to them. If, for example, they had run from problems in the past, they would continue to do the same. I wanted to provide these people with the opportunity to change their lives. I believed the concepts I had learned could make this possible.

My continuous involvement with Lou Tice and the concepts of Self-Image Psychology had a tremendous effect on me. The constant repetition of positive affirmations was beginning to change my way of thinking. I felt strongly that these concepts could effect positive change in both the staff and inmates who worked with me. If you could open people's eyes to new ideas and new ways of thinking, you could teach them to deal with their conflicts in a constructive manner. I believed that if you gave them opportunities and responsibilities, these kinds of positive changes could take place. I decided the best way to achieve this kind of change was to expose these people to the concepts the way I had been exposed, through seminars.

I had the idea of beginning each quarter with a seminar on Self-Image Psychology. Unfortunately, it didn't seem to interest anyone but me. There were no funds and no suitable location available. I wanted to duplicate my own experience as closely as possible. This meant finding a facility that would accommodate thirty convicts for a weekend retreat. The idea of getting approval from the state never entered my mind. I located a Christian Conference Center on Hood Canal, near Seattle. There were cabins that nestled among a forest of green pines and a large conference center that also served as the dining room: it was perfect.

We arrived at the conference center on Friday afternoon, a caravan of automobiles loaded with luggage and excited convicts. I had explained the purpose of the weekend seminar and my expectations of staff and inmates. All had agreed to abide by the guidelines that had been set. The cabins were designed to accommodate four people. Most of the thirty inmates were men, but we had just brought five women into the program from the state's prison for women. We got everyone settled in cabins and set up the conference center for the seminar. Lou Tice had agreed to conduct the program for me.

19. Violence Relived

We were scheduled to begin at 7:00 p.m. It had taken a great deal of effort to put the seminar together. I'd raised three thousand dollars from real estate agencies, insurance agencies and other businesses in the Seattle area. No one had ever tried anything like this before and there was a question regarding the legalities of convicts being allowed to stay in such a location. My intent was to offer them what I felt were the best tools available to change their lives. I was comfortable with the decision and felt that I could handle any concerns or problems that might arise.

Lou arrived at about 6:30 p.m., and we began to assemble in the conference center. I'd purchased note pads and pens and had name cards on the tables. When everyone was seated, I began my introduction. "You all have some idea of why we're here. About a year ago I went through a seminar conducted by Lou Tice from The Pacific Institute. The information had more impact on me than anything in my life. When I decided to accept the position as project director, my first goal was to share what I had gained with you." I suddenly realized that some of the inmates were missing. Son-of-a-bitch, there were four empty chairs. Two guys and two of the ladies who'd just arrived from Purdy were not there. "Let me turn the session over to Lou Tice." I hurried out. The two parole officers assigned by the state followed me. "Shit, there's four inmates missing." I began to search the cabins, afraid of what I would find.

The sound of laughter greeted me as I approached the last cabin. Anger surged through me as I threw the door open. They were all there, leaning back on the beds. The smell of marijuana filled the room. "What the hell are you guys doing?" I snapped. I moved into the room with the two parole officers right behind me. The women had jumped up and were straightening their clothes. The two guys had been in the project for a while. Both had caused problems in the past, but I liked them. "What the fuck you doin, Randy. Shit, man, you know better." He was red-headed, in his mid-twenties, and had a bad drug problem. The other guy was an angry young man named Bill, who was always in trouble with authority. He had a tendency to be a bully, but I liked him anyway.

I backed them both against the wall, the anger and frustration causing me to poke my finger against their chests as I chewed them out. I pushed too far and Bill struck out. His clenched fist smashed into my face. I ripped a left hook to his chin and he slumped against the wall. As soon as I threw the punch, I knew it was wrong. I grabbed him to keep him from throwing more punches. The women were screaming and the parole officers were in a state of panic.

"C'mon, Gordy, knock it off. You'll get yourself in a hell of a jam." I knew they were right.

Bill had stopped struggling and I turned him loose. His jaw was swelling and I could feel a trickle of blood running down my face. For a minute I felt like I was back in prison and a cold fear gripped me. I turned to the parole officers. "You take the women and Randy back to the seminar. Bill and I'll be there in a minute."

"Don't start another beef." The parole officer's voice sounded anxious.

"We're just going to talk for a minute and cool off." I put my hand on Bill's shoulder and we walked outside. The night was clear and you could see the moon reflected in the dark, cool water. We walked along, not saying anything.

The rage I had felt was all too familiar. It painfully reminded me of another time in my life when I allowed rage to control reason. My mind raced back across the years.

It had happened about ten years before. I was in Canada scheduled to fight the eighth fight of my professional boxing career. We
were at Exhibition Park in Vancouver.

The dressing room was alive with activity. Preliminary fighters
were not worthy of a private dressing room. Only the main-event
fighters were awarded such a privilege. I was sharing the sparsely fur-
nished cubicle with three other fighters. Each of us had secured a section of the room for himself as far away from each other as we could
possibly get. I'd managed to get the rubbing table and two chairs in
my area of the room. The other fighters had each found a bench or a
couple of chairs to give their corners a look of respectability.

I was sitting on the rubdown table and Bob Wark, my manager,
was wrapping my hands. I'd been paroled from prison about six
months earlier to pursue a career as a professional fighter. I was still
unbeaten and had won seven fights by knockouts. The fights had all
been four- and six-round matches. My biggest payday had been
$500. I was still involved in illegal activities to supplement my income
but planned to quit stealing as soon as I'd reached main-event status.

We had been in Vancouver for about a week. I'd been partying
and not really taking my training too seriously. I'd met a couple of
ladies and we'd been spending our nights on Granville and Hastings
Streets, raising hell until the early morning hours.

My opponent was a black dude I knew I could beat. He was a light
heavyweight. I was giving up a few pounds, but I knew the guy had a
weak belly and not much heart.

My manager finished wrapping my hands and began preparing one
of the other fighters who was set for a six rounder. I'd gotten the
eight round semi-main. This was the best spot I had drawn on a card
thus far. If I won I'd be in a position for a main event. That is where
all the glory is, the main event: newspapers, cameras and a
policeman at your door keeping the fans away from your private
dressing room.

The fight game is a lot like prison. It is a world where a premium is
paid for physical violence. The fight game is predominantly a man's

domain. There is no softness or love in a gym, and dishonesty is commonplace. There are always ex-convicts to relate to.

The boxing world consists largely of society's poor. Poverty and pain are a part of professional boxing just as they are a part of prison. The fight game is dominated by blacks and other minorities who are manipulated by slick managers and promoters. It is world filled with losers, and many wind up in our prisons. Drugs are used freely by those who frequent the gym. Men in boxing, like those in prison, live on dreams. Both are worlds of make-believe. The one element that keeps you hanging on is the "Rocky Syndrome." One big caper, one big fight and I can be somebody. Where else can society's losers find a moment of glory?

They had just called the six-round fighter to the ring. Bob went out with his satchel of swabs, tape, vaseline and a secret concoction he had you drink if you were running out of gas. It tasted like hell, but it sure did bring you back to life.

"Gordy, when they come for you, just come to the blue corner of the ring. I'll meet you there," Bob hollered out to me as he followed the fighter through the door. I could hear the sound of the crowd. Butterflies came to life in my belly as I anticipated my up-coming confrontation.

I had just started to loosen up when the dressing room door opened. Six or seven guys came bursting into the room.

"How you doin', Gordy?"

"We drove up to watch you knock this sucker out."

"How you been?"

"Shit, man, what's happenin'?" The questions ran together. I was in a state of shock. They were all guys out of the joint.

"What the fuck you guys doin' up here? How'd you get across the border?"

"Hell, man, we told 'em we were comin' up to watch the fight." John Bateman was speaking. He had been a friend in Monroe and the Walls, but I hadn't seen him for a couple of years.

"Where you been? I haven't seen you in a long time."

"Been down in California fuckin' around, but things got hot, so I came back." They were all dressed in trench coats and looked like a bunch of gangsters. I was glad to see them.

"You guys spending the night up here?" I asked John.

"Yeah, we're gonna drive back tomorrow. I gotta report to my parole officer."

"Let's go out and party soon as the fight's over. I'll knock this guy out early and we'll hit Hastings. I've met a couple of ladies and there's a lot of action in this city. There's guys and chicks dealing 'shit' on the street corners."

An usher came through the door carrying a pair of red Everlast boxing gloves in his hand. "Okay, Graham, you're on. Here's your gloves. Just follow me."

"Shit, what happened to Dennis?" (He was the guy who had gone on a few minutes earlier.)

"He got stopped in the first round." The usher sounded disgusted. All the guys were slapping me on the back.

"Let's go, Gordy."

"Knock that sucker out."

"Good luck, man."

I didn't feel right. I hadn't loosened up, and my mind had forgotten the fight. I started bouncing on my toes and throwing punches, trying to get loose. We went down the aisle toward the ring. The crowd was still booing the last fight. Nice reception, I thought.

The auditorium looked like it was almost full. Son-of-a-bitch, why didn't I get ready? I felt the fear in my gut, not fear of my opponent, but fear of the crowd. What if I don't win?

We climbed up into the ring. The ring lights were bright. My eyes burned from the smoky haze that hung above the ring like a fog. I was standing outside the ring talking. The grey canvas on the ring floor was splattered with blood and water. The boards under the canvas rattled as I jumped up and down, trying to get rid of the tension that had come over me. Bob slid a pan of resin under the bottom rope. I could feel the resin. It felt like fine gravel through the thin leather soles of my boxing shoes. I twisted and turned, grinding the resin under my feet. The ring looked slippery and the resin would give my shoes a better grip on the canvas. Bob pulled the stiff leather gloves over my tightly wrapped hands. He pushed the padding away from the knuckles, kneading it up toward the wrist. Then, holding the padding, he cinched the laces down, leaving only a thin layer of leather covering the knuckle area. "How do they feel?" Bob held his palms out and I threw some punches, left, right, left, right, snapping against his hands.

"They feel good."

My opponent was in the ring. His "seconds" were putting on his gloves. He was a tall, light-skinned black with a lantern jaw. He had a soft-looking body and I knew that a good left hook to the belly would put him down.

The ring announcer climbed through the ropes, microphone in his hand. "Ladies and gentlemen, this will be an eight-round semi-main event in the light heavyweight division." The words came out slowly, like thick honey, and then snapped at the end. "In the red corner, at 176 pounds, from Vancouver, Canada, Jack 'The Giant Killer' Taylor. There was a round of applause. "From Seattle, Washington, in the blue corner, at 166 pounds, Gordon 'Gordy' Graham." I raised my hands and bounded up and down as I moved to the center of the ring for the referee's instructions. As the referee went through his routine, I stared at the soft flesh just above the white band of Taylor's trunks. That's where I want to nail him. The referee finished and we went back to our corners to await the bell.

Bob slapped a last minute glob of vaseline on my face and slipped the rubber mouthpiece between my lips. I bit down hard. The stiff rubber tasted like stale antiseptic. I felt Bob's hand slap against my rump and his voice was saying, "Go get him." The sharp clang of the bell sounded, beginning the fight. I moved out toward the center of the ring. We met and I jabbed lightly; the blow glanced off his gloves. He backed up. I moved in, throwing a left hand followed by a hard right that bounced off his shoulder. He moved back again and I followed. I leaned in to throw a left hook to the body when a sharp right hand dropped me to the canvas. I bounced up. Shit, I was down. The referee was counting. I tried angrily to get at Taylor, but the ref held me back and continued his count. When he reached the count of eight, he wiped my gloves against his shirt and motioned us in. Anger at the thought of the bastard knocking me down caused me to throw caution to the wind. I walked in throwing punches. I started another left hook to the body. I was down from another hard right to the jaw. I jumped to my feet and charged across the ring. The referee was waving me off. He was stopping the fight! I must have cut him; why else would he stop it? The referee moved across the ring and raised Taylor's hand. That dirty bastard! I grabbed the ref by the arm.

"What you doin', man? I'm not hurt. Shit, I can knock him out!" The referee jerked free.

"You're over-matched. I'm stopping it."

"No, you son-of-a-bitch, you can't stop it. I'm unbeaten. I'm not hurt." I pushed the ref into the ropes. The red fire of anger consumed me. The anger erupted and I threw a right hand at the referee. We stood toe to toe, slamming punches at each other. I could feel his bare knuckles rip my face.

The auditorium was bedlam. Men were climbing into the ring. Two guys grabbed me from behind and pulled me off the referee. He continued to pummel me with lefts and rights. I kicked out, the anger running wild: frustration, guilt, stupidity, lack of training, parties . . . what the fuck, I must want to be in prison. I felt someone jerking me away. It was John Bateman. I saw all my partners in the ring, fighting their way through the mass of bodies.

"Let's kick these fuckin' Canucks asses," someone screamed. John knocked one of the guys down who'd been holding my arms. Then someone had him by the neck, dragging him to the canvas.

The auditorium was now completely wild, fights were breaking out in the stands and people were throwing bottles into the ring. The riot at Monroe flashed across the screen of my mind. The fuckin' world is crazy! The kid who'd fought the six-rounder before me was trying to climb into the ring to help. Someone grabbed his trunks and ripped them off his body. There he was, stark naked; only his boxing shoes remained. The white cheeks of his ass gleamed as he frantically fought through the crowd.

Finally, the auditorium began to return to normal. The Canadian Mounted Police were beginning to restore order. They had me by the arms. "Get the hell out of the ring," one of them ordered. I climbed through the ropes. People were cheering and cursing me. My mind was spinning. How the hell did I get into this mess? I tried not to think of my lack of training and the dressing room scene. Photographers were flashing pictures and someone hollered from up in the stands, "What is it, a mug shot?" I saw the guy who'd made the remark and the anger erupted again. I charged into the stands after him.

"You bastard, I'll give you a mug shot!"

Before I could get to him, the police had hold of me. "C'mon, Graham, you've got yourself in enough trouble."

I let them lead me down the steps, pushing their way through the crowd. I began to get a grip on my anger. The senseless outburst had left me weak. Man, you can sure fuck up a career. I felt helpless.

John and the other dudes joined me. They were all shouting and reliving the bedlam. "Man, you can start some shit!" They were laughing and slapping each other.

"Bob's really hot, Gordy. He said you're crazy." John sounded concerned. "He said they're holding up your purse."

"Man, that's all he's concerned about." I was still angry. "Shit, they shouldn't have stopped the fight. I wasn't hurt."

The dressing room was full of reporters and people who wanted to see the maniac at close range. A member of the Boxing Commission was there. He informed me that they had decided to fine me. He said they were also considering taking my boxing license and barring me from Canada for life. "I don't give a shit. You gotta lousy system anyway. You stop a fight before a guy is even hurt. That fuckin' ref ruined my career!"

Slowly the people emptied the dressing room. John and my partners stayed on. I showered and packed my gear.

The senseless violence of prisons, the memories of being hurt and of hurting others, the ache from broken bones and scars slammed into my consciousness.

As Bill and I walked across the green, sloping lawn in Seabeck, the old fears ran wild. No more. I can't live like that. I've got to develop discipline.

I gripped Bill's shoulder and said, "I'm sorry, man. Let's go back to the conference center and in the morning we'll have your jaw x-rayed."

"I think it's broke. It hurts like hell."

We walked into the seminar, blood dripping down my face and Bill's jaw discolored and swollen. Some way to begin a class on mental health, I thought!

The state parole officers were really upset. "The director of the project in a fist fight with one of the inmates. If we don't report it, and Bill or one of the other inmates turns you in, it's our ass." Pete was worried. He was a big laid-back parole officer and a decent guy.

I felt sorry for him. "You have to do whatever you feel is right, Pete. I wish it hadn't happened, but it did. When Bill threw a punch, my old habits just took over. My mistake was jamming him into a corner, especially with women present. I'd probably do what he did under the same circumstances."

The incident was reported, but there were no repercussions. We returned to the University of Washington Sunday evening. The seminar had been a real experience and an eye-opener for most of the inmates in attendance. It developed a solid base to work from for my staff, and I continued the practice of Self-Image Seminars for the balance of my tenure as director.

20. Convicts Can Change

I continued to study and develop my teaching skills. The university provided an excellent opportunity for me to further my education. Psychology, philosophy and management principles consumed me. My mind was set on teaching these concepts. After one year of directing the project at the University of Washington, I resigned and went to work full time for Lou Tice and The Pacific Institute.

I was still a controversial figure in the state, but there were two or three correctional leaders who were willing to give me a chance. Bob Rhay, the warden at Walla Walla, who'd been my keeper for three years, and Edna Goodrich, the warden at the women's prison at Purdy, gave me the support I needed. They offered me the opportunity to share the concepts with inmates in their respective institutions.

I knew that the Self-Image Seminars were not an answer in themselves, but I also knew that many of the men and women in prisons were a lot like me. They'd gotten caught up in the Walt Disney world of prison life, and change was no longer seen as an option. As a lecturer for The Pacific Institute, I was now in a position to open their minds so they could see that there were options. I couldn't wait to get started. At last I'd be doing what I knew I was meant to do.

That first seminar in Walla Walla was the realization of a dream. There were fifty inmates gathered together in a classroom in the education department. Many of them were former partners of mine; some I'd celled with. They all knew me personally or by reputation. There were blacks, chicanos, Indians and whites. Few knew what to expect, and a large number felt I was running another game on the Man.

The seminar began. As I made my initial introduction, many of the inmates were slouched back in their chairs half asleep. But as the information unfolded, I could see them begin to sit up, and one by one they began opening their note pads and starting to write. By noon they were excited. "Man, you got some heavy shit here." "How the hell did you learn all this?" The questions came from all directions.

It was early afternoon and I was explaining the concepts of self-image and Comfort Zones. "The self-image, or picture of the truth, becomes a controlling mechanism. It works like any other controlling mechanism. If you set a thermostat at 70 degrees, the temperature doesn't remain at 70 degrees. If it did, the heating and cooling mechanisms would kick on and off continuously and they'd burn out rapidly. To avoid this, they've created a dead space where neither mechanism need be on. So if the temperature rises say to 73 degrees, an electrical impulse is sent to the cooling mechanism that drops the temperature down. If it drops to 67 degrees, there is an electrical impulse sent to the heating mechanism that brings the temperature back up. You and I operate in a similar manner. The thermostat is our self-image, and we also have a dead space where we function quite well. However, we are not electrically controlled, but tension and anxiety controlled."

"Every time we get away from where we feel like we belong, we start getting feedback that tells us we're out of place. One of the things that occurs is the stomach begins to secrete more digestive juices. We also get up tight in the upper part of our bodies, making it difficult to use our skills. We don't think clearly. The free flow of information is cut off from the subconscious to the conscious. It's like preparing all year to go to the parole board. You get your story down, then you get in the board room with two people across the table from you who hold your freedom in their hands. All the things you were planning to say won't come out. As soon as you get out of the room, you remember ten things you wanted to tell them.'' I could see heads nod all around the room.

"There are times when your vocal chords tighten and your voice gets squeaky. This happens when you lie. Another thing that happens is moisture occurs immediately on the surface of the skin. All of these things occur when we try hard to change, or try to be different from what we see ourselves to be. It's no wonder we have trouble making even minor changes, much less changing total life styles. When this feedback takes place, our first tendency is to get back where we feel comfortable. If we can't go back, then we look around for people who are like us, think like us, talk like us and sometimes look like us. This could be a social group or an individual. Think about the last time you were with a group of 'square johns.' Were you out of your Comfort Zone? A Comfort Zone is violated when people or teams who see themselves as losers start winning. They get up tight and will creatively work to get back to where they see themselves to be. Now here's the bottom line: I believe that prisons become a Comfort Zone. We adjust to the abnormal environment of a prison for survival's sake. We become effective in this culture, and the longer we're here, the more difficult it is to make it on the outside. I look at the stupid things that brought me back to prison. I knew I was smarter than that, but I believe it was a subconscious desire to get out of the stress and pressure of being in the free world.'' The room was deathly quiet. I looked around and I felt they knew I was right.

"What the hell can we do about it, man?'' a young black guy asked. His voice sounded angry, but I knew he just felt trapped.

"I'm going to give you some tools that I've used and that work if you apply them.''

It was late in the second day of the seminar. The inmates were totally caught up in the information. I'd poured a ton of energy into the sessions and had been bombarded with questions at every break. I felt drained. The needs were so many. Some of the inmates had life sentences facing them. There are few answers that have meaning. All you can do is let them know you care. We'd talked about the importance of accepting accountability for your own decisions, of recognizing that there are choices even in prison.

"It is important that we begin to accept accountability for our future and stop waiting for someone else to make it happen for us. Many of us fix the blame for who we are on the police for patrolling at the wrong time, a bad lawyer, or a 'fall partner,' and it gets so vague. Some of us lay the blame on society or our childhoods. There may be some truth in this, but generally we're responsible. Most of us are in prison for being thieves or lawbreakers. The important thing is to get out and stay out, to make your life work for you."

That first seminar at Walla Walla had a dramatic impact on many of the inmates who attended. A self-help group was formed to reinforce and follow through on what had been learned. This became an ongoing program within Walla Walla. Many of the original seminar attendees are out of prison, doing very well as honest citizens. The experience was another milestone in my life. I was on my way. There was no going back.

21. The Rescue

McNeil Island is a fifteen-minute boat ride from Steilacoom, a small town in Washington State. It is a beautiful island with much of its natural beauty protected from tourists and land developers by the federal penitentiary which spirals against the skyline. The miles of dark green water surrounding McNeil serve as an added security measure for the twelve hundred inmates confined in huge cell blocks. The prison is old and has the infamous feature of housing as many as ten men to a cell. It is one of the oldest prisons in the federal system and also one of the most secure.

I had been conducting staff training programs at the island, and the warden had become a good friend. He'd asked me to conduct a class as part of the pre-release program at the prison. The program was designed to better equip inmates to make the transition from a controlled environment to free society.

There were about fifty inmates in the classroom. Some I recognized from the period of my life when I was doing time at Walla Walla. Those who knew me nodded guardedly, and I could sense that they weren't sure what I was doing there and didn't want to blow my game. I sat down on a table at the front of the room while the warden began his introduction to the group.

He began explaining that the pre-release program was organized to help inmates better adjust to society. "Some of you will stay out, but one of every three will be back. So look at the man sitting on each side of you. Which one will be the man who comes back?"

I could see the inmates shifting nervously in their chairs. The warden continued, "We are fortunate to have with us today one of the best trainers I've ever met. He has done a lot of training for my staff and has agreed to conduct this program on his own time. He is also a very good personal friend of mine."

I saw the inmates who knew me looking around for the person the warden was introducing. There was no way they could imagine me being the warden's friend. "Let me introduce Gordy Graham of The Pacific Institute." I kept watching the guys who knew me. They sat straight up in their chairs like they'd been hit with a bucket of ice water.

I walked to the large green chalkboard and picked up a piece of chalk. "How are you guys doin'? I know what you're thinking. This pre-release is a bunch of junk, but I gotta be here to get out. Who cares about how to buy a house or how to get insurance. When I went to pre-release, I used to find a chair where I could sleep. Hell, I knew it wasn't relevant to the challenges I faced. Some of you know me. In fact, I see some guys out there that I've walked the 'big yard' with. How ya'all been? How you doin', Dick? Man, you mean they're gonna let you out? What are these joints comin' to?" We all laughed.

I could feel the inmates relax and begin to listen. "You know, I've gotten out of joints about five times legally and a couple of times illegally." They laughed. "But you know, I always goal set just to get out, not to stay out. How about you? How do you see your life one year from today?" My eyes scanned the room. Son-of-a-bitch, there's Joe. I didn't even know he was here. His thick glasses brought back memories of cold nights in Idaho. "What the hell you doin' here, man? When you gettin' out? I know you can relate to goal setting just to get out of prison. We've been there, right?" He nodded. I could sense his anxiety at being released from prison. He doesn't have a chance of making it. He doesn't have any survival skills.

My mind flashed to the cold November day, some years ago, when Joe and I had escaped from Walla Walla. We'd pulled off one of the slickest escapes ever executed from inside the Walls. Most of the escapes made from prisons are meticulously planned. They are timed down to the second. Some are thought out and even charted for years. But most of the guys who plan the escape, or do escape, have one common problem—they don't plan beyond the walls. Seldom do you exceed your expectations—I knew that now. We'd goal set to escape and from then on it had been like a keystone cop operation. My eyes met Joe's and I knew he was thinking of the same experience. My mind jumped back to the cold barn not far from the prison where we had waited for darkness to conceal our movements.

It had started to get dark inside the barn. I crawled out of the warmth of the hay and walked to the doors. I slid one of them open just far enough to peer out. The rain had stopped. The sky was a dull grey and darkness was settling over the bleak rolling fields. I could see lights in the distance. It must be a farm. It was too dark for the search planes to see us from the air, and I was anxious to get moving.

"Let's go, Joe. It's almost dark," I said.

I could hear him moving around in the hay. "I'll be with you in a minute," was his response.

"C'mon man," I urged.

"I lost my glasses again," he moaned.

I bit my lip in silent frustration as I walked over to where he was on his hands and knees searching.

"Son-of-a-bitch! How in the hell did you lose them this time?" I remarked as I got down beside Joe and sifted through the loose hay. The barn was pitch black and the only way to find the glasses was to feel around in the hay.

"Where did you set them down?" I asked.

"I didn't. They must have fallen off when I was sleeping."

"I know one thing. When we find them this time we're gonna tie them son-of-a-bitches on you," I said in mock anger.

I took a book of matches out of my pocket and lit one. My hands shook with the cold that was beginning to overwhelm my body. The small flame flickered as I moved it back and forth over the area where Joe had slept.

I looked at Joe in the dim light. He looked wild. His hair was filled with chaff and strands of hay. His eyes were wild and dark against his pale drawn face. I could imagine what I must have looked like and thought that right now we sure didn't look dangerous to anyone but ourselves.

The strain of the escape plus the hunger and cold made me feel depressed. I felt as if I were in a hopeless situation. We couldn't go back. We couldn't stay here. And there really wasn't anywhere to go. Now Joe and his damn glasses. How the hell can I take care of a practically blind guy and myself too?

"I found them!" Joe shouted. I could see him in the darkness, holding the glasses in his shivering hands.

"Hold on to the goddam things, for chrissake," I said as I got up off my knees. "Let's get the hell outa here before something else happens."

I slid open the barn door and stepped out into the night air. There was a whistling wind driving the cold across the fields. It cut through my clothes.

I hesitated for a moment. The barn seemed inviting.

That helpless fear tugged at me again. I felt trapped. Where are we going? How? Why? I shook the fear and closed my mind.

"Let's head for those lights, Joe. We might be able to steal a car."

We started out across the muddy fields, stopping only to scrape the caked mud from our shoes. The lights were closer now, and the dark outlines of buildings were beginning to take shape. We crossed a paved road that wound through the fields. A gravel driveway led to the cluster of farm buildings that nestled among a few tall trees. I could see four vehicles parked around the buildings. There were no lights showing in the farmhouse, but there was a large floodlight on the front of what appeared to be a barn.

"I don't think there's anyone home, or they're already in bed," I said to Joe.

"Today's Thanksgiving, man. They're probably gone for the holiday," he answered. "Let's see if we can steal one of those rigs."

"Okay," I said, "but stay out of the light just in case someone is home."

We walked quietly up along the edge of the driveway until we were in the farm yard directly across from one of the vehicles that was parked under a large maple tree. It was a fairly new pick-up truck.

I slipped into the shadows of the big maple and crept up to the pick-up. I tried the door. It was unlocked! I eased the door open and slipped inside. Damn, the keys were in the ignition!

I waved to Joe to get in the other side of the truck. I slid under the wheel and softly closed the door. Joe got in and eased his door shut. I pumped the accelerator and turned the key. The motor sputtered once and then roared to life. I put it in gear and moved out onto the gravel driveway. We drove slowly up the driveway. The wet gravel crunched under the pick-up's tires. The noises of the truck sounded loud. I turned around to see if we had aroused anyone in the house, but it was still dark.

When we reached the paved highway, I pulled the light switch and the darkness opened up before us. I hesitated at the highway and then turned to the right, hoping that was east.

"Find the heater, Joe, and turn that bastard on full blast," I said as I reached over to turn on the radio.

I found a station that was playing country and western music. The heater was beginning to warm up the cab of the pick-up and for the first time since we'd escaped from the joint, I felt warm and comfortable.

There was no traffic and I kept the pick-up rolling along at about sixty. I checked the gas gauge. The tank was half full.

"We're gonna have to get some gas to get to Montana," I informed Joe.

The radio interrupted our thoughts: "It's eleven o'clock and time for the news. The top story at this hour is the two convicts who escaped from the maximum security unit of the Washington State Penitentiary at Walla Walla. Officals are still not saying how the two managed to escape and there has been no word on their whereabouts.

The two, Gordon Graham, serving twelve years for armed robbery in Spokane, and Joe Nichols, serving twenty years for bank robbery, are considered extremely dangerous and should be approached with caution. They are believed to be wearing prison clothes and headed for Seattle. Anyone with information on the two should call the local authorities.''

Joe was the first to speak. "I sure don't feel extremely dangerous, do you?''

I looked over at him. He had his coat off and was holding it in front of the heater. He looked anything but dangerous. The green sign at the junction pointed the way to Spokane. We turned in that direction and the pick-up rolled along the wet pavement.

"We'll head for Montana. We should be able to find a service station on the outskirts of Spokane and fill the tank. Also, we had better stop somewhere and switch license plates before long, 'cause they're gonna know we stole this truck soon as those farmers find out it's gone.''

The pick-up was warm. The raspy voice of Merle Haggard trying to coax some lady into his arms came over the radio.

We rolled through the night, putting miles between us and the penitentiary. The twelve o'clock report came and went with much the same information as before. I knew that inmates would be listening to the news flashes back in the Walls. We carried their hopes and dreams with us. We'd beaten the joint. They would be rooting for us, following the news as avidly as if it were the Super Bowl! I could feel their excitement as they anxiously awaited the next reports on our progress.

We had a responsibility to succeed. We couldn't let all of those guys down. Our own discomfort and the potential danger became almost secondary issues. My cell partners would be laughing it up. We'd beaten the Man.

The lights of a small town brought me back. I looked at the gas gauge. We needed fuel if we were going to make it to Montana.

"This is more like it," I said over the sound of the soothing music, "those wheat fields were kicking my ass." Joe nodded in agreement.

"I was thinking that we better not stop in Spokane, Joe, 'cause the cops are really going to be looking for us in that area. Maybe we can make it to Idaho and gas up there."

The gas gauge still registered about a quarter full.

Joe's hoarse voice echoed my thoughts when he mentioned that he was hungry. "We ain't ate for almost three days," he said.

"Yeah, maybe we can get something when we stop for gas," I nodded. I hadn't thought about food for a long time. The cold and the constant fear had shut out everything. Now, sitting in the warmth of the truck, I could feel the gnawing hunger in my belly.

A light snow was beginning to fall when we crossed the state line into Idaho. A sign said that the town of Kellogg, Idaho, was eleven miles down the highway. I just hoped that there was a gas station open in Kellogg. We were going to need a full tank to make it over the mountain pass to Montana. I sure didn't want to run out of gas on this highway, not with the snow coming down harder now.

We looked for a sign that would indicate that there would be a gas station in the town. Joe spotted a red and blue sign that promised twenty-four hour service. We took the exit off the highway.

The service station had two pumps. I pulled the pick-up in beside the pump labeled "regular" and switched off the engine. A sleepy-eyed attendant came out of the small building that sat off to the side. He pulled a black and red mackinaw over his shoulders as he strolled over to us. I rolled down the window and told him to fill it up.

As the attendant started to get the gas hose, I noticed the lights of a car slowly pulling in behind us. At first, I didn't realize the significance of the markings on the car, but then it rapidly dawned on me. Police!

"Son-of-a-bitch, there's a cop behind us! Let's get the hell out of here!" I heard myself say.

I threw the pick-up in gear. It leaped forward, the half-inserted gas nozzle falling to the ground. We careened out onto the street, sliding wildly on the slippery blanket of snow.

I fought the steering wheel, trying to hold the truck on the street. The police car was less than a block behind us, its red light flashing and slicing through the sheet of whiteness that was falling around us.

I knew we would never lose the police car unless we made a run for it on foot. "We better dump the pick-up and make a run for it, Joe," I said. "I'll take a left at the next street and pull it over."

We hit the corner, sliding out of control across the intersection, bouncing off the curb on the other side. I jerked violently and the pick-up slid back across the street.

"We're gonna hit that pole!" I yelled as the pick-up wildly skidded sideways across the icy streets.

The rear end of the pick-up slammed up against the pole and spun us around. The engine quit. I figured that we had better run for it on foot.

"Let's go, man!" I hollered to Joe as I jumped out of the cab.

We ran around a corner of a building that looked like a school. We fought for balance in the snow as we kept running. We rounded another corner and were back at the pick-up parked against the telephone pole.

There wasn't any sign of the cops, so I suggested that we had better get our coats out of the pick-up. We dashed across the street to the truck, grabbed our coats and took off down an alley. We reached a fence and climbed over it. We kept running, stumbling and falling in the snow until we were both out of breath. Cold air stabbed painfully at my lungs.

"Man, we got to get someplace to hide. They'll have every son-of-a-bitch in the town out looking for us with guns."

Joe pointed at some long grey buildings in the distance and suggested we head for them. We started off toward the factory buildings, stopping to peek warily around the corners for signs of the police.

After slipping and sliding through dark streets and alleyways, we crossed the lighted main street, jumped a fence, scrambled down an embankment, and crossed some railroad tracks that ran parallel to the buildings. We ran between the tracks and buildings until we came to a half-open door.

We slid through the opening and inched our way along in the darkened room. Gradually my eyes adjusted to the darkness and we found ourselves in a gloomy, uninhabited smelter. We continued walking. The farther we went, the warmer it became. I bumped into what seemed to be a huge boiler.

"I think we're in the boiler room, Joe." I could feel the heat radiating from the sides.

"Yeah," Joe answered, "at least we found someplace to hide that's warm."

I suggested that we hole up until they stopped looking for us. I eased myself to the warm cement floor. I rolled up my coat for a pillow and stretched out in the warm darkness. Joe did the same. The warmth of the room made my eyes heavy. My body felt drained from the running and the tension. I was totally exhausted, both mentally and physically. I dozed off into a warm, comfortable sleep.

The clickety-clacking sound of a passing train jerked me out of my sleep.

I nudged Joe awake. "Hey, man, there's a train passing. Let's see if we can jump it and get the hell out of this town."

I jumped up, put on my coat and started for the exit. "C'mon, Joe, let's go before we miss it," I urged.

He was rummaging around on the floor and before he said it, I knew. "I can't find my glasses," he said in a sorrowful low voice.

There was no use getting upset this time, but I did spit out some choice expletives that had to do with the heritage of Joe and his troublesome glasses. I knelt down beside him and began helping him search. All the while I could hear the train passing by the building.

"We gotta hurry, man, or we'll miss the goddam train," I pleaded. I felt like grabbing Joe and shaking him.

Finally Joe exclaimed, in a voice that sounded as if he had struck gold, that he had found them. But it was too late; the train was gone and the only things we could hear were the dwindling train noises and our heavy breathing.

"There's got to be another one along soon," Joe pleaded.

In a not-too-friendly voice I said, "Hang on to those damn glasses for just once on this goddam trip."

Why did I bring Joe along? One of these damn times those glasses are going to do us in.

A few hours later we heard another train coming by the smelter.

I turned to Joe. "Do you have your glasses?" I asked. He said he did. We went to the door, opened it a little and peered out. It was daylight.

The train was only thirty yards away from where we were, traveling at a very slow speed. There were a dozen freight cars being pulled behind a noisy steam engine. I nodded at Joe and we ran alongside the train until we came to a boxcar with its door open. I jumped up into it and reached down and helped Joe. The train began to pick up speed. I stood up and looked around the interior of the boxcar. It was empty and the floor was covered with bits and pieces of bark and wood.

"This ought to take us into Montana." I tried to sound cheerful. I was damn glad to put some miles between us and Kellogg. Joe huddled in one of the corners of the boxcar shivering, his knees pulled up against his chest to keep warm. The engine was four cars in front of us and we could hear the steady beat of puffing steam as it wound its way through the snowy countryside.

There was no sign of life, just trees and rolling hills that seemed cold and remote in the grey light of afternoon. As we clipped along, I thought of Rita. Hell, she may not even live in Missoula now, and knowing her, she sure as hell will have some dude living with her. Maybe we can get her to lend us some money. Then we could take a bus out of Missoula. They won't be looking for us there. I didn't want to say anything to Joe.

The train seemed to be slowing down. Why the hell would they be stopping out here in the middle of nowhere? I stood up and leaned out the door. There was nothing in sight. Just snow and the shiny metal railroad track that ran around the side of a small ridge and out of sight. I could see the engine ahead of us and the chimney that stuck out of the caboose about six or eight cars back. They sure as hell can't be looking for us out here in this desolate place.

I sat back down beside Joe. "What the hell they slowing down for?'' Joe asked.

"Don't know, man. Ain't nothing but trees and snow out there,'' I said with puzzlement in my voice too. The metal wheels had slowed and you could hear them click as they rolled along. The cars seemed to veer to the right. I stood up and leaned out of the car. I could see smoke coming from the trees ahead of us. The train had left the main track. We were pulling onto a siding. I could see stacks of freshly cut lumber and a cluster of wooden buildings begin to emerge from the trees.

"Shit, man, this is a fucking siding!'' I could hear the brakes as they slowly brought the train to a halt. Voices sounded and I could hear the cars being unhooked from the engine. "Son-of-a-bitch, this is a logging camp. Man, we better get the hell out of here!'' I jumped down from the boxcar. Joe followed. As we ran along the track, I could hear voices yelling, "Who the hell is that? Hey, where you guys goin'?'' We just kept running. Our exhaustion and cold bodies were forgotten as fear drove us on. I glanced back and could see loggers pointing and hollering at us to stop.

We were out of sight. "Man, I gotta rest. I can't go no further.'' Joe's voice was gasping.

"Okay, let's stop, but you know they'll have cops looking for us within hours. We gotta get the hell out of here! They gotta know who we are. How many guys you seen running out here in prison clothes?'' We started running again. I could see Joe's face grimace with pain as he ran and I knew his leg was hurting him. "Let's walk, man. If you hear anything, get off the tracks and out of sight. We got to stick to the railroad or we'll get lost in these fucking mountains. I sure as hell don't want to freeze to death out here!''

Darkness had begun slowly closing in on us like the lid of a coffin shutting off the light. The cold was almost unbearable as we trudged along the railroad track. Every hundred yards or so we'd run a ways, trying to fight the bitter cold that turned our feet to ice. The wind ripped at our bodies and froze our faces. "Shit, man, we gotta start a fire or we'll freeze.'' My face felt like it was cracking when I talked. I looked down the track, and in the distance I thought I saw a light.

"Did you see a light, Joe?"

"No, I didn't see nothin'." Joe's voice sounded weak and I felt sorry for him. Then I saw it again. I knew it was a house or something ahead of us.

"Man, there's a light up there. There's got to be buildings or somethin' that we can hide in to get out of this cold. Let's run a ways."

"I can't run, Gordy. My leg is killing me and I think my feet are frozen."

"Okay, man, but you gotta keep goin'. If we stop we'll freeze for sure. See if you can walk a little faster. I know there's something up there." We walked faster and I reached out to help Joe as we stumbled through the night. More lights came into view and an excitement ran through my body. "Man, it's a town. Maybe we can get a car." I thought of the warm pick-up we'd wrecked in Kellogg. Just to be warm again—even the prison cell would be better than freezing out here in the mountains.

I pulled Joe along. The thought of a warm car or building that could provide shelter from this merciless cold made me want to run, but I couldn't leave Joe.

This tiny community was comprised of only two or three houses and a tall, dark building that looked like a church. The houses, with bright lights shining from the windows and smoke curling from their chimneys, brought tears to my eyes. Geez, why can't I live like that. I fought back the tears and turned to the dark barn-like building. "That must be a church, man. Let's see if we can get inside."

"Let's take one of the houses and make the people drive us out of here." Joe sounded desperate.

"No, man. I don't want a kidnapping charge. Let's see what's in the church first."

A gravel road ran up a hill to the dark building. As we walked closer, I could see a cross at the top of the sloping roof. Suddenly I felt fear run through me, but the cold drove us on and I locked the fear out.

It seemed that in my most difficult hours, God was always present, causing me to face my inabilities; it made me angry and scared at the same time. We crossed the snowy yard leading to the church. A sign in front said "The Cataldo Mission." The nearest house was two or three hundred yards away. It was dark and silent as we went up the wooden stairs to the double doors leading into the mission. "Son-of-a-bitch, it's locked. Shit, I didn't think they locked churches."

"Let's try the windows." We moved around the side of the building to a window. I pushed the window upward and it slid open.

"C'mon, Joe, this window's open. You step in my hands and you can slide through." I cupped my hands and made a step. Joe put one foot in my hands and reached up to the opening. He pulled himself up and wriggled through the window. I could hear him as he hit the floor on the inside.

"Man, it's a dark son-of-a-bitch. I can't see a fuckin' thing." His voice sounded muffled. I reached up and grabbed the window sill. My body ached as I pulled myself up to the opening. I eased through and dropped to the floor beside Joe. It was dark and cold.

"I'll light a match, Joe, and we can see where we are." I reached into my pocket and found the book of matches I'd placed there before we left the prison. My hands were shaking from the cold. I used three matches before I finally managed to get one lit. I cupped my hands around the small orange flame until it was burning well. The tiny flame cast a dim light that outlined rows of pews. "We're in the chapel. Let's see if there's a candle." I made my way down the aisle to the front of the room. The match died and I lit another one. I could see an image of Christ on the Cross at the front of the chapel. It felt errie. The flickering flame bounced off the white figure of the Lord. I spotted candles on what appeared to be an organ. Just then my match died. I lit another match and took one of the candles from the holder on the organ and placed the flame to the wick of the candle.

The flame from the candle seemed bright in the darkness and I shielded it with my body. I could see more clearly the rows of wooden pews. At the rear of the chapel was a door that led into another room. "Let's check back here, Joe, and see if there's any food or a stove.'' We made our way down the aisle, through the door, into the back of the church.

There were a range, a refrigerator and cupboards in the room we entered. ''Son-of-a-bitch, let's see if there's anything we can eat.'' Joe pulled the door of the refrigerator open and the light came on. It was empty except for an ice cream carton and half a loaf of bread. I pulled the ice cream out and opened the top. It was almost half full of yellowish-brown ice cream that had dried from age. Joe had taken out the bread. We moved to the range and set our finds on the counter. We began searching the cupboards. They were filled with plates, cups and glasses, but no food. We pulled drawers open and found pots, pans and silverware, but no food. ''Let's see if we can get this oven going and get some heat.'' I held the candle so I could read the writing on the knobs. I turned the one that said ''oven'' to 400 degrees and opened the door.

The coils began to glow orange and then red. You could feel the warmth beginning to work its way through the cold. Joe and I crowded as close to the oven as we could get. We stuck our hands inside. Needle-like pains ran up my arms as the heat penetrated the cold in my hands.

The room was cold. While the front of me was being warmed by the heat of the oven, my back stayed frozen. We both kept turning, first warming the front and then the back. The heat felt good.

''I'm gonna put my shoes in the oven, man. My feet are so cold I think they're frozen.'' Joe was sitting on the floor in front of the stove, untying the ankle-high shoes. ''Help me pull them off, Gordy. They're stuck.'' I reached down and worked the shoes off his feet. His socks were worn through and there were huge blisters on both feet.

''Son-of-a-bitch, man, your feet are blistered! How the hell have you been walking?'' I placed his shoes on the oven door. How the hell is he going to make it? I looked at Joe. He seemed frail and helpless. Damn! What the hell are we gonna do?

''Let's toast some bread, man.'' I took a handful of the dry, hard bread slices and spread them on the metal rack in the oven. ''We might as well try some of the ice cream.'' I got two bowls from the cupboard and searched through the drawers until I found spoons. I filled the bowls with the dry ice cream and handed one to Joe.

It had been almost three days since we'd eaten. The sweet taste of the stale ice cream was delicious. We pulled the hot slices of bread from the oven and piled the rubbery ice cream on the hard bread. ''Man, do you know this is our Thanksgiving dinner?'' Joe sounded better. The cold was beginning to disappear and there was hope in his voice.

''Yeah, man, turkey couldn't taste any better. We better see if we can get a couple hours of sleep 'cause we're gonna have to get out of here before daylight. Let me see if I can find anything to cover up with.'' I picked up the candle and began searching through the cupboards. There were a number of robes hanging in a closet. I took them back to the stove. ''We can make a bed out of these, but we better take turns sleeping 'cause if we both go to sleep, we may not wake up. You go ahead and get some sleep first, Joe.'' I spread the robes out in front of the oven and Joe lay down. My eyes were heavy, but the cold kept me awake.

The night wore on and I dozed. When I opened my eyes, the grey dawn was beginning to seep through the windows. I reached over and shook Joe's shoulder. ''We better get moving, man. It'll be daylight before long.'' Joe rolled over and sat up.

''Son-of-a-bitch, I'm sore. I don't know if I can walk.'' His shoes were still on the oven door, and I reached over and handed them to him.

''Better get these on. We'll take it easy and see if we can reach a town or someplace where we can get hold of a car.''

The back door had a bar across it and I pulled it free. The cold chill of the morning hit me smack in the face when I pushed open the door. ''Boy, it's a cold bastard!'' It was hard not to stay by the heat of the oven, but I knew we had to keep moving or we'd get busted.

I could see the dark houses in the distance as we started along the railroad tracks. ''There's no way we can steal a car here. They'd set up roadblocks and nail us before we got twenty miles.'' I knew Joe wanted to, but we'd be in trouble or be forced to hurt someone, and I didn't want that to happen.

Joe was limping badly. I knew his feet must be killing him, but we couldn't stop. The cold had driven out the warmth and my body shivered from the chill. "Son-of-a-bitch, it's cold. It must be ten below zero." Joe didn't answer.

We trudged along. The tracks seemed to go on forever. It was afternoon and we'd been walking for hours without seeing any sign of life. We were both numb from fatigue and cold. Every mile or so we'd rest, but it was too cold to stop for any length of time. Each time we rested, we cursed the cold and grudgingly forced ourselves to our feet, each step an effort. Pain was etched on Joe's face and I knew he was near exhaustion. I knew it was hopeless. There was no way we were going to be able to get out of these mountains. The police had to know where we were and it was just a matter of time before they located us. It was hard to understand how we could get a four hour start on the cops and wind up in such a helpless situation. I'd never quit or admit that we were beaten, but the truth was there and it kept gnawing at me.

It was almost dark. We were entering a portion of track that ran through a cut in a small wooded hill. Trees and bushes grew along both sides of the track, making their way up the sloping hillside. We were mentally and physically exhausted. Neither of us had spoken for miles. Thoughts of spending another night in this cold, God-forsaken land kept running through my mind. We could freeze to death if we couldn't get a fire started, which was highly unlikely since everything was covered with snow. I was worried about Joe. He was in pain and spent. I knew he couldn't go much farther.

We stumbled along, heads down, forcing our legs to move. We had no thought of where we were or where we were going. We only knew we had to keep moving.

I heard a limb snap, but it didn't register. My mind was dull with fatigue. Suddenly the hillside erupted with men and guns! "Hold it right there! On your bellies. Don't move. Get those hands up!" Shrill orders were being screamed from every direction.

The trees and bushes were alive with people. Some were dressed in red coats and hats, some in police uniforms and some in greens; where the hell did they all come from? I stood with my arms raised over my head. One move and we're dead, I thought. I wasn't scared. In fact, it was almost a relief. Joe had fallen to the ground and lay there on his belly. "Get your ass down, you son-of-a-bitch." I felt the sharp metal jabbing me in the back and I fell on the cold ground. There were guns everywhere I looked. Gaping barrels of shot guns stared ominously in my direction. Shining rifle barrels were glaring in the fading light and pistols held tightly in shaking hands were a constant threat.

You could sense the excitement running through their veins. The stalkers, after all, had captured two dangerous escaped convicts and their emotions were reaping the spoils. What they didn't realize was that it was more of a rescue than a capture.

They shook us down and cuffed our hands tightly behind our backs. "Okay, let's go." We were marched up a narrow trail to a dirt road where a dozen vehicles waited. We were shoved into the back seats of two separate police cars. After our captors exchanged "slap on the back" congratulations and "way to go's," we started the journey back to Walla Walla. My thoughts turned to Whitey and the other guys who had helped us escape. We had let them down. Shit, we should have made it. I felt a sense of guilt at not trying harder. I should have gotten shot in the capture, or at least I should have made a run for it.

The warmth of the car heater felt good and my eyes got heavy as the car rolled away.

My eyes focused on Joe in the seminar room. He and I had planned to escape, and we had. We had not planned how to live "outside," and we couldn't. Now he would face that outside world again.

It's insane to let a guy like Joe out without some support system. He's gonna steal. Hell, that's all he knows.

22. A Visit to Prison

The Pacific Institute became my life, both personally and professionally. For seven years I was consumed by the concepts and techniques of Self-Image Psychology. We had grown from a two-man operation, Lou Tice and me, to a corporation with over forty people, all actively involved in marketing our seminars. I'd become the National Sales Manager and a respected leader in the teaching and marketing of Self-Image Psychology Seminars.

Janie and I had developed close personal relationships with most of the people at "T.P.I." They were our friends and we shared many good times together. They all knew my background in prison, but they also knew me for what I had become: an honest, caring, high-performance member of society, a man with a strong sense of social commitment. The staff ranged from former pro athletes to former lawyers. We had former Catholic priests and former convicts, all with one thing in common: the desire to influence positive change in our society.

The people at The Pacific Institute were always supportive of our prison work. They accepted without question those "funny looking people" I always had hanging around me. The staff accepted me on faith, yet I still felt a need to share some of where I'd come from with them. It was with this idea in mind that I decided to take all of The Pacific Institute people to prison.

The T.P.I. staff members were accustomed to three-piece suits, pretty dresses and Caesar salads. Their lives were far removed from the prison environment. I believed that an inside look at prisons would have a great impact on them and make them aware of another world. I wanted them to have the opportunity to visit six-wing and to get a feel for the prison world and the people who lived there.

I called the warden at Walla Walla and suggested the idea of T.P.I.'s staff visiting the prison. He gave me permission and we began to make plans for the trip. I contacted friends of mine who were still inmates in Walla Walla and told them of my intent. They got excited about the idea and decided to set up a program that would involve inmate speakers and a tour of the institution. John Bateman, a leader in an inmate self-help group, began to coordinate the activities within the prison.

At that time, Walla Walla was in a state of unrest. I was warned that the Walls could easily become another "Attica." A series of violent assaults and inmate disturbances had disrupted the delicate balance that controls the prison world. I'd heard rumors that riots were certain and that a hostage situation was possible. I contacted John and expressed my concern about bringing thirty people into the Walls under these conditions.

His reponse was definite. "Man, we'll take care of your people. I'll get the heads of the inmate clubs together and get their support. We'll assign someone to each person you bring, so nobody will bother 'em!"

"I'd appreciate it, John, if you'd tell them I'm chartering two planes to bring over a bunch of people who are important to me. I want our people to know where I came from and that there's a lot of guys like me in prisons throughout the country. These are people who care. They've supported our work in prisons for the last six years."

John told me he understood and assured me he would see to it that everything would be handled.

Janie had made arrangements through a local airline to charter two sixteen-passenger planes. Ron Medved, a former professional football player, had invited two of his friends, but the rest of the group were all T.P.I. staff. We had a total of thirty-one people.

It was a beautiful clear day when we left Seattle. The Cascade Mountain Range, peaceful and green, spread out beneath us. The lushness of forest began to fade and to be replaced by the familiar patchwork of wheat fields and rocky brown desert signaling "Walla Walla country."

We landed at the Walla Walla airport and were met by a group of Seventh Day Adventists who'd volunteered their time to work with inmate groups in the penitentiary. They had secured two vans to transport us to the prison. I spent most of the trip worrying about the day's outcome.

Man, I hope there ain't no problems, I thought to myself. My nerves were tingling. This was like a fantasy! Gordy Graham chartering planes to bring thirty respectable citizens into Walla Walla to spend a day with the convicts. Only in America!

I was glad Ron Medved, the former pro-football player, was with me. He had become a special friend and was supportive of me and this project. He'd brought Fred Forsberg, another former N.F.L. player, who'd been the defensive captain for the Denver Broncos. The guys in the joint had a lot of respect for pro athletes. I knew they'd enjoy spending time with Ron and Fred.

Fred was affectionately called "Fantastic Freddy" and was a person who enjoyed life and the excitement of new experiences. His laugh, which was rarely absent, was like a hearty red wine that stimulates everyone.

I was anxious to share all of these people with my friends in prison.

The laughter and conversation in the vans came to an abrupt halt as the ominous walls of the penitentiary came into sight. "They'll want to shake us down and you probably won't be able to take your purses inside," I informed the group. About half the people with me were women, and I could sense their uneasiness.

"The guys inside are friends of mine and they have our day all laid out. It will be a good education for you and it is something most people never experience," I tried to reassure everyone. I remembered my first view of Walla Walla through the narrow windows of the Green Hornet, and I knew how they must have felt.

The guard at the security gate was pleasant. He had a memo with all of our names. He asked the women to leave their purses in the security booth. He checked each person's I.D. as he called our names. When we had all been properly identified, we were allowed to enter the security area that separated the administration building from the prison. There we were required to pass through a metal detector. It took awhile before we could all pass inspection. After numerous trips back and forth through the finely tuned detector, belts, watches, coins, and, in some cases, shoes, were piled on the table. This protective measure was a recent addition to prison security, a result of the frequent stabbings and the violent actions of radical group members.

A number of inmate leaders had joined us in the security area. It felt like "old home week."

"How you doin', Gordy."

"Man, it's good to see you."

"We've got everything handled."

After the hellos were over, we got down to the business at hand. John Bateman outlined the day's activities for us. We were scheduled to visit all the ethnic clubs. We were to have lunch and dinner in the inmate dining hall and a program had been prepared that was to take place in the Lifers' Club.

I called John and the other inmate leaders aside. "I'm going to turn things over to you guys. The women are a little nervous, so make sure they don't get jammed by some 'rapo.' I don't want a bunch of guys putting 'the bum' on these people. They're my friends. I want them to get the message that people in prisons are still people."

A member of the chicano group spoke up. "Don't sweat it, man. You've been our 'bro' and we'll take care of them, no problem."

"Let's go, John." I joined the group and the guard opened the huge metal door.

We stepped into another life.

I thought of the first time I'd gone through that opening with Bob Schwarder. Bob had died of an overdose of drugs in Chicago a couple of years earlier. He had been feeding a drug habit he'd developed behind the Walls.

The warden had given me free access to the institution. There were no correctional officers assigned, only the inmate chaperons. Inmates lined the walk-way as we crossed the institution grounds. Muscular upper bodies, shirtless and gleaming with perspiration, were on display for the visitors. It gave the institution the appearance of a pirate settlement. As we walked along, I noticed one of our chaperons gently placing himself between an over-zealous convict and one of our group. I was glad to see the inmates taking their job seriously. It reassured me to know that my people were being protected.

We were taken to the "awareness tier" located in "Big Red." One end of Big Red, a long brick building, served as a maximum security prison within a maximum security prison. Its purpose was to isolate dangerous inmates from the main population. There was also a section that housed those who needed protective custody: inmates who had testified against other inmates, were suspected of being informants, or had failed to pay a debt. The other end of Big Red housed two or three groups of inmates who were in social therapy programs. The Awareness Club had formed after a seminar I'd taught in Walla Walla. Inmates had secured permission to form a self-help group through which they could cell together to continue the practice and use of the concepts and techniques taught in my seminars. John Bateman had become one of the primary leaders of this group.

We assembled in the narrow tier that ran the length of the cell block. Chairs had been arranged and we all found seats. One by one, the inmate leaders stood to welcome us to Walla Walla. Since institutions are political battlegrounds, each separate faction needed recognition and time to express its viewpoint.

There was a lot of tension in the joint. I could feel it when I talked to the inmates. Changes in the administration, cutbacks on inmates' freedoms, and a general feeling of helplessness had created a dangerous situation. I was having second thoughts about our timing for the visit. Prison had become more volatile over the years. I wasn't sure how much control Bateman and his friends had over the younger population.

First, John, the president of the Black Prisoners' Forum, spoke. He was followed by the chicano leader and then the president of the United Indians of All Tribes. The minister from the Black Muslims greeted us and joined in the welcome.

When the inmates had completed their welcoming remarks, I asked all of the people with me to introduce themselves. I could sense the nervous tension in many of the voices as each person stood and gave his or her name and company position. I wondered if they realized that the same nervous tension was a part of what an inmate felt when he tried to adjust to the outside world. I hoped they would come to understand this.

We were escorted through the prison grounds and into one of the huge cell blocks. Inmates were sent ahead to check the area for potential problems. The call "women on the tier" alerted the men in the cells and allowed them time to get their acts together. My nerves were on edge, and I kept my eyes moving constantly, watching for signs of trouble.

At lunch time, we were escorted to the inmate dining room. The chaperons paired off with my people as they went through the chow line. Inmates serving behind the steam tables were in a state of shock. The joint was full of beautiful ladies and men in suits and ties. I could see them glancing at each other. Their eyes were saying, "What the fuck is happening?" Inmates who'd been in prison for years without a visit were getting whiplash checking to see if they were dreaming. It had to have been a real mindblower to suddenly have their world invaded by "funny looking" people from the streets.

The inmate chaperons were having a ball! The ladies were escorted proudly to their tables, their hosts glancing casually at the less fortunate inmates, a knowing smile beaming across their faces. "Yeah, man, I'm a player. I've been telling you I was cool." They were enjoying their moments in the sun.

After lunch, we began a tour of the various inmate clubs. Each group had somehow secured its own turf. This had been a gradual change. It was a result of the political awareness that had swept America during the late sixties and early seventies. The administration had been attacked by outside advocacy groups and the American Civil Liberties Union (ACLU). Inmates had ridden the crest of this movement to freedoms heretofore unheard of in penitentiaries.

The amount of space in each group's private meeting area depended on political power and aggressive leadership. The clubs were decorated with a strong flair for revolutionary figures: Che Guevara, Malcolm X, Geronimo and others adorned the walls. Statements that screamed freedom, revolution, and peace were generously scattered around the rooms. Each group had a strong message delivered by the elected leader. Every message contained a plea for help and understanding. After each meeting, I would lose two or three of our people, usually Ron Medved and "Fantastic Freddy" Forsberg. It took me fifteen minutes to get them out of the Black Prisoners' Forum. Freddy's laugh could be heard throughout the joint. The convicts loved him. Hell, they fit right in, I thought. The group surrounding Ron and Freddie continued to grow. They acquired quite a fan club.

The afternoon passed rapidly and it was chow time again. If there is going to be trouble in the joint, chow time is usually when it starts. I didn't like the idea of sweating through another meal, but there was no way to avoid the situation. The relationship between visitor and inmate had been firmly established. Dinner went smoothly and I felt relieved. We still had the program in the Lifers' Club scheduled for the evening, but I felt better. It looked as though this day might conclude without an incident.

That night we walked through Lifers' Park, well-manicured and complete with fish pond and wooden bridge. Winding stairs led to a large meeting room. The darkness on the stairs and the memories of knife assaults sent chills through me. Freddy's laughter brought me back to reality and I tried to shake the fear, but it persisted. The room was full, with inmates standing in the back. All of our people were seated in the front of the room, escorts firmly entrenched beside them.

John Bateman opened the program by introducing me, explaining why we had intruded on their world at Walla Walla. Each leader, black, brown, and white, advocated political power for his group. When I was called upon to speak, I expressed my excitement at returning to the Walls with a group of friends from "that other world." I wanted to impress the inmates with the idea that change is possible. "You guys know that it could just as well be me sitting out there. I just happened to get exposed to some concepts and techniques that turned my life around. I've also been fortunate to have people around me who allowed me the opportunity to change. These people have never looked at who I used to be, only what I could be."

I wanted so much to penetrate their protective armour and get them to see. When I had finished speaking, my wife, Janie, was asked to say something. She walked to the front of the room, her small size emphasized within this group. The inmates knew that Janie was my strength. When she finished speaking, they rose to their feet, and their appreciation echoed through the room. I could see that Janie was very moved by the demonstration.

The tour, the program, the special interaction between inmates and my staff had come to an end. Our day in Walla Walla was over. Good-bys had been tear-filled and promises to write and "see you when I get out" followed us through the gate and into the security area. I was drained. My body felt like I'd been in a sauna for hours. Along with the exhaustion was a feeling of accomplishment. Ron and Freddy had made friends everywhere they went. Their athletic backgrounds and their love for people had made a special impact on the population. Each of the women had received addresses from the inmates, but I'd discouraged them from giving anyone their phone numbers. I knew how lonely incarceration could be, and I didn't want them barraged with phone calls.

The comments flowed as we soared across the state. They ranged from "Man, there are a lot of good guys in there" to specific questions about certain inmates. The experience had changed these people's opinions about inmates and prisons. The objective had been met.

Ron and Freddy were laughing and talking about Dave and John like they were old friends. It felt good. I leaned back in my seat. Man, I thought, they'll be talking about this on six-wing tonight. Weariness took over and I dozed off.

23. Turning Loose

After eight exciting years with The Pacific Institute, Janie and I decided it was time to step out on our own. Lou Tice had been a strong influence over the years. We'd traveled across the country together teaching seminars. Our range of clients had grown to include government agencies, military leadership and athletic teams. National real estate firms, the automobile industry and many of the *Fortune* five hundred companies were using our services. The Institute was now reaching into other countries: Canada, Australia, England. Lou Tice had arrived. We had expanded from live teaching to the production of internationally marketed videotape training programs. Due to costs of production and overhead, prices for our products had continued to rise. "Live" training had gotten more expensive, but the demand for our seminars continued to grow.

Because I had been part of this exciting period of growth, the decision to separate from T.P.I. and form an independent corporation was one of the most difficult decisions of my life. I struggled with options that would allow me to continue as a part of the Institute. After several months of deliberation, it was clear that it wouldn't work.

Janie and I met with Lou Tice in our conference room to discuss alternatives. We'd been together so long and had accomplished so much. It had been nine years earlier when we first decided to form a partnership and take on the correctional system of America. A former high school coach and an ex-convict: not a very promising combination for such a massive undertaking. But over the years we'd become one of the most respected training companies in the correctional world. I'd taught courses in over a hundred prisons. We had implemented our videotape training programs in almost every federal prison in the country and in a large number of state facilities. We'd contracted with the state of Washington to operate our own community prison. We'd hired many men and women just released from prison. Though some were back in prison and others were dead, many had become successful members of society. Wardens, associate wardens and directors had become our close friends. We were invited as guest speakers to national conventions. We had climbed our mountain.

Lou had become very successful. A large, spacious house on Lake Washington and a Cadillac limousine were now a part of his world. I was comfortable in this world, but memories of six-wing and a growing awareness that I was somehow losing my original purpose wouldn't leave me alone. I had come to a crossroad in my life and my path was leading in a different direction.

I looked at Lou across the conference table. He had a few more grey hairs. More expensive suits were visible indications of the success he had experienced. Otherwise, he was pretty much the same Lou I had met years earlier.

Because of his powerful personality, The Pacific Institute was Lou Tice. It would always be Lou Tice. My identity had become so intertwined with Lou's that it was difficult to determine where he ended and I began. I had to find out what Gordon Graham could accomplish on his own. Janie had sensed this much earlier, but she had waited patiently for me to realize it.

"Well, Lou, I guess you know that I've been considering a change. I've decided to separate from T.P.I. and form my own corporation." Lou was silent for a moment. "If you're going to do it, then you might as well do it right. I'll have George work out the details." George was our corporate manager, a former basketball coach and a long time friend of Lou's. We talked for a few minutes, both of us anxious to end the meeting.

I had cemented my decision. It was over. I felt relieved, sad and scared all at the same time. Relieved that I'd made the decision, sad to leave people who had been so much a part of my life, and scared at the prospect of being on my own.

My mind slipped back to just a few of the intense experiences of the previous eight years.

At Purdy Treatment Center in 1972, I had given my first full seminar—to an all women's group—two powerful experiences combined their impact.

There had been forty women inmates in the room. Their eyes followed me as I walked to the chalkboard located at the front of the long oval classroom. I could feel the tension in my belly and the perspiration turning my hands clammy. I silently talked to myself, beating back the fear. "You're a very effective teacher and have energy and enthusiasm when you teach." I tried hard to visualize myself as an effective teacher, but the fact that it was my first full seminar and that I was scared, kept fighting for my consciousness.

I'd spent long hours in preparation, laying out the session plan on flip charts. I reviewed the examples and visual aids that I'd been using, making affirmations about my abilities and my confidence. But now it was "showtime." I had to deliver a seminar to forty women prisoners who were not thrilled about their participation.

Edna Goodrich, the warden at the women's prison in Washington State, had agreed to a contract to conduct a series of seminars for inmates at her institution. Though I'd been able to convince others of my ability and confidence, I hadn't done such a good selling job on myself. I was scared. Most of the examples I'd picked up from Lou Tice and from my own experiences were about men. The athletic examples were all males. I tried to think of some great women athletes, but my mind was blank. What kind of jobs do you talk about? I knew they had a school for beauticians, but you can't keep talking about beauty school. How does it feel to be a mother in prison? I knew how it felt to be a father, but did mothers feel differently? What kind of activities did women participate in while they were in prison? Did they make "pruno," did they mess with drugs, did they get in fights, were there gangs? How many homosexuals were there? I realized that I really hadn't done as much homework as I thought I had.

Did the women hurt the same? Did they dream of their men and their kids? Did they develop anger and hostility toward society? I was sure they did all of the same kinds of things, but they might do them differently. Were they starved for love and softness, for gentleness? Did they suffocate with these needs? In addition to these serious matters, my nervousness touched other areas.

I had on a sport coat and tie. I'd spent some time in deciding what to wear. The choices were rather limited, but I did have a suit and three or four different sport coats to select from. I wanted to look professional, but I also wanted to look sharp. The old images were still there: forty women, man, you've got to look sharp!

I picked up a piece of chalk and turned to face my audience. "I'm Gordy Graham from The Pacific Institute." Forty faces, smiles, knowing glances, boredom, hostility, desire, skepticism all greeted me. The urge to run, to plead illness, ran through me. I brushed my hand across the fly of my pants to assure myself that I was zipped. I continued, "The seminar that we are going to go through has nothing to do with prisons or inmates. It is a seminar that has to do with getting our lives together. It applies to all people. Bankers, professional athletes, real estate agents, insurance people, all go through the same seminar. However, I will try to use examples that you can relate to. I've done seventeen years as a consumer of correctional services." I could sense the shifting in chairs and the knowing glances that indicated, "This dude knows what's happenin'."

By the time the seminar had ended, I walked out of Purdy with a powerful experience that supported my belief that I could teach the concepts of Self-Image Psychology to women as well as men. My *awareness expanded in the area of women's rights, and I began to see what we do to enhance or detract from the image of women and the women themselves in our society. Prior to this experience, I had thought of women only as mothers, wives or objects of sexual desire. Now I understood and felt the frustration of women who had tried to fill various roles and had failed to adjust, women who rejected the roles entirely, and women who wanted to fill the roles but had made lousy decisions in selecting their partners. It was a significant growth step for me. I would never again try to place women into traditional molds.*

At McNeil Island in the summer of 1973, the room had been anything but ideal. It was long and narrow, with barely room for people to squeeze between the wall and the folding tables that had been set up in an elongated "U" shape. A chalkboard was positioned at the front of the room. There were no windows in the cement walls and the July heat had turned the room into an oven. It was late afternoon and the seminar was just getting under way.

I had been introduced by the warden as an instructor from The Pacific Institute. We had contracted to do some staff training and to put a pilot group of inmates through a seminar.

I had taught three or four seminars at Purdy and one at Walla Walla. My confidence was increasing, but this was a group of adult males, many with degrees and some who'd been lawyers and businessmen on the "streets." The one comfort I experienced came from the three or four inmates I'd done time with who were in the session. They'd lend credibility to me as a person. My belief in myself had gotten stronger and I could sense an increase in self-esteem. It was much easier to deal with the anxieties. I had developed a technique that helped me prepare. I'd flick my mind back to one of the seminars at Purdy and the great feelings that I'd gotten from doing a good job. Then I would project into my next seminar and feel the same emotion. This allowed me to get more and more comfortable in my presentations.

"I'm Gordy Graham, Vice President of The Pacific Institute. We provide training seminars across the country in business, industry, education, athletics and corrections. The seminars have nothing to do with prisons or prisoners. The seminar consists of concepts and techniques that increase personal effectiveness. I don't profess to be an expert at anything. I do have some common experiences that might help me relate to you. In my life I've done approximately seventeen years in prison. At one time in my life I did 365 days on bread and water. Some of you know me. You know that when I was doing time I was a 'good convict.' "

"I was president of the resident council and a leader in prison. I've escaped from prison, I've been shot and stabbed, and there are not many things that you've done that I can't relate to. The seminar we're going to share changed my life. You may find something that will turn on the lights for you like it did for me." The room was silent. There were fifty convicts in the hot, stuffy room and they were hooked. The more honest I could be about my past, the more attention I gained for the concepts that had helped me.

Some inmates would leave the seminar with a new awareness; lights would be turned on and the darkness pushed backwards. Some would be consumed by the concepts they had learned. Some would take small segments and apply them to specific areas of their lives. Some would leave feeling, "Gordy's got a hell of a thing going." Some would hurry to their cells and stick needles in their arms or cheat someone in a card game or a business deal.

Whatever these sophisticated adult males had been and might choose to become, I could meet them on their own ground and offer them the possibilities I had had.

At McNeil Island in 1974, I had taught my first group of staff people: "I don't know, man. I don't know if they'll listen to me." The staff program that we'd presented had so far been taught by Lou Tice. It had been very successful and had received a lot of positive feedback. We'd grown as a company and someone else needed to teach in this area. That was to be my assignment. The warden at McNeil and the executive staff knew me and my background. I'd taught a number of inmate seminars and had developed a feeling of confidence in that area. My background gave me credibility and established a firm identity with the inmate population, but dealing with staff was different. Staff members have a definite attitude about ex-cons and the examples that I had grown comfortable with were no longer appropriate. I knew that I would need to establish myself as an honest, caring person before I would dare share my background. I needed to establish credibility and an expertise in teaching or they'd eat me alive.

My introduction neglected my years in prison. I introduced myself as Vice President of The Pacific Institute and explained the seminar's purpose: "The program is not designed to tell people how to do their jobs. We assume that you are experts in the area of corrections. What this seminar can do is share ideas on how to use your skills more effectively, how to reach your career goals more rapidly, how to make your life work better for you—in a sense, 'How to get out of your own way.' " I could feel the tension beginning to ease. I continued to fire information at them.

By the morning of the second day of the seminar, we were comfortable together. My examples about prisons and prisoners were becoming more personal. I was discussing restrictive motivation and how people who live their lives feeling like they have to do things have really given up accountability. "People who are on this side of the motivational scale develop a philosophy that reduces to this: 'It's not my fault.' They fix the blame on others for their failures. It can get so vague that they fix the blame on society. Prisons are full of such individuals. They fix the blame on a lawyer, a judge, a fall partner and give up total accountability for the act that got them into prison. I lived a major portion of my life fixing the blame on others. For seventeen years of my life I was a consumer of correctional services."

I could see the remark gradually begin to register. "At one time I did 365 calendar days on bread and water." The room was silent. Then one or two of the people began to laugh. I guess the thought of an ex-con teaching the Man struck them as funny. I could see their point. The mood shifted and I knew it was going to be all right.

It would have been easy for them to reject the information I gave because I was an ex-con, but the crowd that gathered around me at the break was friendly and curious.

"I knew you had to be an ex-con or a former staff person because you knew too much about prisons."

"Where'd you do time?"

"How did you change? What caused you to get into this?" The questions flew. I tried to answer them as best I could. There was a feeling of acceptance and respect in the group and I felt good about it.

My confidence grew and I began to use examples from my past. I could see the excitement in their faces as I touched on challenges that they faced daily. There were hard-line correctional staff people in the seminar. They were the ones I felt were getting the most from the session. We were on the same wave length. They knew that I knew and cared about who they were and had empathy for the challenges that they faced. We could talk about certain aspects of a prison that no one else could understand. The majority cared about people. They had gotten into corrections for the right reasons, but gradually the idealism had been eroded and they'd lost their belief in themselves and in people. Constantly faced with failure, they seldom had the opportunity to experience success. They saw men and women they had invested time and emotions in fail and return to prison. The knowledge and awareness that I had developed over the years allowed me to share insights about their world that they had never heard before. The realization that this was where I could be most valuable came as a real shock to me.

We met at the warden's house after the seminar. The warden's house boy, an inmate, was a friend of mine from Walla Walla. The warden introduced us, and I could see the look of amazement on his face. He had known me as a convict, a leader in the prison environment. To see me as the guest of honor in the warden's house must have been an absolute mindblower! *"How you doin', Red? How much time you got?"*

It was in 1978 that I had first worked at Folsom Prison, California's maximum security institution. Ominous grey stone walls cut a stark circular path along the green rolling hills. A cloak of loneliness seemed to lock out the outside world. The words from the song *"Folsom Prison Blues,"* made famous by Johnny Cash, ran through my mind. This place would definitely give you the blues, I thought.

I parked by rented car in the visitors' parking lot, took out my black suitcase, locked my car, and walked over to the security shack that nestled comfortably among the green maples. Two blue-uniformed guards were checking in visitors. I waited patiently until they had finished. I smiled at one of the guards and asked directions to the training center. He had me sign my name in a large dog-eared visitors' log and grudgingly pointed to a long grey building that sat under a huge maple tree on the side of a sloping green hillside.

The silent unfriendly attitude of the two guards brought back unpleasant memories of other maximum security prisons. "Outsiders" were viewed with suspicion and in some cases outright hostility. The constant threat of escapes, drugs being smuggled into the prison, lawsuits, inmate unrest, political scrutiny, and unrealistic expectations by society and inmates alike, had led to the mistrust that pervades correctional institutions.

On my way up the hill, I felt a tingling fear in my belly. I'd been teaching seminars in the California prison system for the past year. I'd heard that the Folsom staff members were tough, hard-nosed correctional people. Prisons develop reputations and Folsom is seen as the "end of the line," a "tough joint for tough convicts."

How do you teach change when people have lost their belief that change is possible? My seminars were structured to encourage constructive, positive attitudes towards ourselves and other people. How do you do this in a negative environment where failure is experienced daily and survival alone is a measurement of success? These thoughts raced through my mind as I climbed the narrow, worn walkway toward the training center.

I had been teaching with The Pacific Institute for six years all over the United States, but every time I started a seminar with correctional staff, anxiety and fear filled me. And Folsom was the toughest challenge of all.

What will this group think when they learn about my past?

How long should I wait before I tell them?

Somehow I always knew when the right time came. My background as a consumer of correctional services is hard for prison staff to accept. But when they realize that I'm honest about who I am and that I'm good at what I do, they begin to let down the barriers created by their negative experiences in correctional institutions.

Prison changes people, but prisons don't change. The inmate gradually develops defense mechanisms for self preservation or escape: withdrawal, hostility, fear, collaboration, participation in gangs or athletics, retreat into protective custody or insanity, and the ultimate—suicide. All are defenses against the prison environment. Scheming ways to beat the Man becomes a way of life in prison.

Correctional staff members, who represent the Man, also change. They may enter the profession with high ideals and a belief in people, but years of constant pressure and continuous exposure to violence and dishonesty narrow their vision and dim their belief. An ex-convict who attempts to penetrate this world as an honest citizen is peceived with jaundiced eyes.

That world is unique. Society has charged correctional people with an almost impossible task. They work in a hostile, negative world with inadequate resources, minimal support from the public, and an almost insensitive ear from political leadership. Change has gradually made their job more and more difficult. Values are no longer clearly defined in our society. Right and wrong are not as easily determined. An influx of disenchanted young men suffering from the impact of the Viet Nam experience has had its impact on the correctional environment. In addition, correctional people are judged not by their successes, but by their failures. Years of effective leadership can be destroyed by one riot. Opposition forms immediately at the first hint of the death penalty being enacted, yet inmates kill each other daily in overcrowded archaic prison environments, and correctional staffs are held accountable. Cries for adequate funding and new, manageable facilities fall on deaf ears until a riot or a hostage situation embarrasses political leadership. Then resources magically appear.

We were well into the morning of the second day at Folsom Prison. The warden and associate warden had loosened up and were involved with the concepts. The fifty staff people were laughing now, and the information seemed to flow without effort. The examples became more and more relevant to their world.

It was break time and the warden, Paul Morris, and I were standing beside the coffee urn. "It's going really well, Gordy. You're hitting some key points." He looked relieved. It had been his decision to bring me into Folsom. I had been working across the country with correctional staff for a number of years, but I knew his anxiety.

"What do you think about me telling them about my past?" I wanted Paul to feel comfortable.

"You make the decision. You've been tracking with them beautifully and they like you." His reassurance made me feel good. Shortly after the break, I told them more about the backgrounds of others at TPI and about my own.

"My background is different. I've worked in education and managed community correctional programs, but for over seventeen years of my life I was a consumer of correctional services. At one time in my life I did 365 days on bread and water."

It took a moment for it to sink in. There was complete silence except for the shifting of chairs as the impact of what I'd said hit them. I was watching the associate warden. If I could get him I'd be okay. His face broke into a smile followed by laughter that spread through the room like wildfire. I breathed a sigh of relief. My own Folsom Prison blues were over.

An incident that had occurred in Oxford, Wisconsin reminded me of many times when the impact of the seminars had been immediate and powerful. There had been a huge black man in the first session we taught at Oxford. He had been deeply influenced by the concepts. He formed a group that worked on reinforcement of the ideas, and each time I returned, Lester was in the seminar. He began to teach the concepts to other inmates. His dedication and honesty impressed me, and I wanted to help him.

When he became eligible for parole, I asked that he be allowed to spend the last thirty days before his release with me in Seattle. The parole board accepted the plan and Lester flew out to Seattle. He moved into my home and I began to develop a plan for him that would give him an identity. He began to teach seminars and to speak at conventions and meetings. Over and over I had had the privilege of witnessing this kind of change.

The kaleidescope of past experiences slowed, and my mind returned to the present. Those had been intense years of growth and change, but it was time to move on.

Janie and I set up the corporate structure. We leased office space, hired a secretary and began to solicit business. My reputation as an instructor was well established in the field of correction. My background no longer created the negative reaction that it once had. I continued my work in corrections and began to move into new areas.

After a number of programs sponsored by state societies for Certified Public Accountants, my presentations received some of the highest evaluations ever given a speaker. I was able to add business seminars to my corrections work. At first it had been difficult to see how I was going to be able to relate to people from the "real world." I had to find ways to relate to them that would cause them to see the traps in their own experiences. They might not relate to prison or doing time in the Hole. Did I know enough about their world? I'd been a father for a while; that would help. I'd faced mortgage payments and the I.R.S. I started on such common ground and soon found other points of reference.

My first seminars with a general audience were powerful experiences. There were no preconceived ideas. The fact that I had been a convict didn't detract from or enhance the presentation. The knowledge that most people are interested in learning and will respond to a positive experience settled me down.

My work with military organizations, especially Navy correctional facilities, was very successful, and The Human Development Training Institute soon expanded in these areas.

My knowledge and experience continued to grow. I was constantly testing new theories and participating in seminars and courses on management styles, motivation, leadership and communications. The Human Development Training Institute was launched and afloat.

Epilogue

After emptying my pockets, removing my watch, and taking off my shoes, I finally passed through the metal detector without setting off the alarm. Security was much tighter here at Monroe than it was at airports, which must make it difficult to carry knives and other weapons. However, I knew the inmates had figured ways to beat the security. With twenty-four hours a day to scheme, it's difficult for the Man to stay ahead of the population that makes up a prison.

Chairs were the only furniture in the long, narrow visiting room. Some had worn red upholstery, others were plain grey metal scarred from continuous use. A lone correctional officer was seated behind a desk at the front of the room, checking visitors as they entered. Most of the visitors were women, many with small children. I thought back to the many times Janie and our children had visited me in the Washington State Penitentiary.

Tony came into the visiting room. He was a big, good looking, young Italian from New York City. He weighed 225 pounds and had tremendous potential as a fighter. While he had been out of prison, he'd won six professional fights—all by knockouts. His career had stalled when his manager could no longer get Tony fights, and he had fallen back into the old habits that almost always led to prison.

We shook hands and found a seat in one corner of the crowded visiting room. Small circles of chairs had been arranged by inmates, each seeking some semblance of privacy. Children were running through the room, laughing and crying, oblivious to the pain and anguish of the parents. The faint smell of disinfectant hung in the air. I could feel the rivulets of perspiration beginning to trickle down my sides.

I looked at Tony. He was only twenty-four years old. He'd already served three years in prison, and unless something could be done to help him, he would do five more years. Over the years I'd tried not to get personally involved with inmates. Most of the people I'd done time with were either out and doing well or they were dead or doing life in a maximum security prison somewhere. If you avoid getting to know the inmates, it is much easier to work in the prison environment. But here I was, back in Monroe, trying to find a way to help this young man who had made very irresponsible decisions about his life.

The visiting room was crowded. People pressed together, shoulders hunched forward in their metal chairs, trying desperately to establish a sense of privacy amid the chaos. Tony and I squeezed into a niche in one corner of the smoke-filled room, causing a series of angry glances from other visitors who had to adjust their chairs to make room for us. They need more room and some ventilation, I thought, as we settled into the folding metal chairs.

"How's it going, Tony? It looks like you're not missing any meals." Tony was a big man and had a tendency to put on weight rapidly when he wasn't training.

"I'm doing okay. Can't get any exercise 'cause we're in our cells most of the time."

He was being held in a section of the institution designed for men who had not yet been sentenced by the court. He'd been arrested six months earlier after getting into an altercation with an alleged drug dealer. He had pleaded guilty to the charges. The judge, after reviewing all of the circumstances of the crime, had made a decision to give Tony another chance. It had taken courage on the judge's part to suspend Tony's sentence. For the judge's consideration and approval, we'd laid out an alternative to prison that would provide a job and participation in a structured treatment program for Tony. He still faced the possibility of being sentenced to prison as a parole violator, but the first hurdle had been overcome. The parole board would review his case within thirty days and either reinstate him on parole or return him to prison as a parole violator. In the meantime, the uncertainty of his future, after being locked up for six-and-a-half months, was beginning to show on his face. There were dark circles under his eyes and a tightness in his face.

I knew how he felt. You have no control over what happens to you during this period of waiting. Your future is held in limbo while a decision is being made. You are at the mercy of the system. The origin of the old adage that "the wheels of justice turn slowly" becomes all too clear.

Hoping that he would get this additional chance, I stressed the importance of Tony's own efforts. "I think there's a good chance that the parole board will go along with the judge. But you've got to make a commitment to discipline your life. There's no way that you can hang around drug users or places where drugs are being used or sold and stay out of trouble. This may be your last chance to make it as a fighter. If you go to prison for three or four years, age will defeat you." I thought of the years I had lost in prison when I was young, the wasted opportunities when people had given me that "one more chance."

I didn't want to see Tony make the same mistakes. He had the potential to be a good fighter. Lack of support and a series of disappointments certainly contributed to his present situation. And I knew just how easy it could be to fall back into old patterns when things don't work out for you, especially if you don't have a strong foundation. Tony would need incredible discipline and commitment to get through the inevitable hard times.

I thought back to the first time I had met him. I had first heard about Tony in early spring of 1981. The Human Development Training Institute was beginning to establish its own identity. There were still many former clients who associated me with The Pacific Institute, but the separation was complete. We had developed a strong videotape training program, "Breaking Barriers," that was beginning to sell. I was on the road teaching live seminars and promoting the Human Development Training Institute.

I'd just returned from a trip to the east coast. John Bateman, one of the guys I'd helped get out of prison, was in my office. He'd been doing some work for H.D.T.I., and we were discussing his progress.

"I met this heavyweight fighter who just got out of Monroe. He and his manager are interested in going to a seminar." John sounded excited.

"What's his name?" Over the years I'd stayed in touch with the fight game, and it still intrigued me.

"Tony Gallo. He's from New York. He started fighting in Monroe for Doc Borenson and won the Golden Gloves last year in Seattle. He's had six pro fights and won them all by knockouts. I don't think Tony's manager knows much about how to deal with guys who've been in prison. I've talked to Tony about you and the seminars. I think it would really help him."

"Why don't you set up a meeting. I'd like to talk with him and see where his head's at before he goes to a seminar. Unless the guy is serious, there's no point in either of us spending a lot of time trying to help him."

John scheduled a meeting for the following week. Tony looked like a fighter. He was big, 6'3'', and looked like he weighed 250 pounds. He was dressed in a dark blue, three-piece, pin-striped suit. A neatly trimmed moustache and black wavy hair gave him the appearance of an oversized Burt Reynolds. Man, if this guy can fight, he's worth a million! An Italian heavyweight following the smash hit *Rocky*. What a natural!

"I'm Gordy Graham. It's nice to meet you." I walked over and shook his hand. He was relaxed and his grip was firm.

"John's talked about you and says you're a fighter. I remember you winning the Golden Gloves last year. You fought for Doc Borenson. He's been at Monroe forever."

Tony had a folder that was full of newspaper clippings and fight pictures. His professional record was six wins and no losses. He'd been fighting preliminary bouts around the Northwest and had established himself as a puncher. He'd been dubbed the "Italian Bear," a take-off on the "Italian Stallion."

Tony described his situation to me. "My last three fights have been cancelled and my manager can't seem to get me fights. It's hard to stay in shape and I need to make some money. When I came out of Monroe, I was in good shape, but now I'm twenty or thirty pounds overweight. I need to get away from the environment I'm in, or I'm going to wind up back in the joint." His voice was sincere and I liked the honesty that came through. He was where I had been twenty years ago. Preliminary fighters don't make any money, and unless you've got connections or money behind you, there's no way you can survive in the fight game.

I wanted to help him.

"Do you want to continue fighting?" I waited for his answer.

"Yes, but only if I can depend on someone getting me fights. My manager is a good guy, but he is doing this part-time. I never know whether I've got a fight and I'm always broke. I'd rather quit than go through any more of that shit." His openness and his sense of the problem impressed me.

"Can you fight?" Most fighters deep down know if they have the ability to be great.

"Yes. I think I can beat most of the heavyweights right now. Give me a decent trainer and a couple or three months and I'll beat anyone. But I've got to get fights." His matter-of-fact manner made me believe him. I'll bet he's a tough son-of-a-bitch.

"Well, let's see if we can get you into condition. I'll call a couple of people and see if I can find a place. Then maybe you can get some financial backing if you're as good as you say. You have all the right ingredients to be a winner. You're a heavyweight, you're Italian, and that's positive after the film *Rocky*, you're a good looking dude, you're articulate and you've got some sense. It seems like someone would invest in your career."

Tony was overweight and in poor physical condition. We decided that he needed to get out of town and work himself back into condition. "If you're going to be a professional fighter, you've got to be willing to sacrifice." These words had been thrown at me over and over when I was young, but I had failed to listen. Tony had agreed to follow whatever program we laid out for him.

I stressed to Tony the need for discipline in attitude as well as exercise: "We've got to find a place that takes you out of your present environment, one that will allow you to get in shape both mentally and physically."

I had a friend named Dave, who lived in a small town at the foot of the Cascade Mountains. He owned some property high in the mountains, miles from civilization. He agreed to let Tony live on his property.

"However," I cautioned Tony, "there are no cabins and the weather is still cold." These facts didn't deter him.

"Get me a tent and I can make it." We secured a small tent, a sleeping bag, and an assortment of camping gear and headed for the mountains. To lose weight, Tony had decided on a strict fruit and vegetable diet. He'd purchased celery, carrots, lettuce, cucumbers, oranges and apples. Dave had commented, "If you can survive on that, you'll be ready to fight grizzly bear!"

We drove Dave's four-wheel-drive to the spot selected for Tony's camp. After unloading the gear, we helped Tony build a fire pit with rocks. It was late afternoon when we finished. The tent was set up and we had constructed a fireplace that would make a boy scout leader proud.

"I think I'll build a fire," Tony declared. He proceeded to stack a pile of large tree limbs in the fire pit. After lighting match after match, it became obvious that Tony had never been a boy scout. We suggested that he chop some dry kindling to get his fire started.

Dave asked, "Have you ever done any camping?"

"No. We never did any camping in the Bronx." Despite his humor, his reply caused me some concern.

"Tony, it's going to get cold up here. You sure you can handle this?"

"I'll be okay. Just bring me some more vegetables and fruit when you come back."

We drove away, leaving Tony miles from town with no transportation and only a tent, sleeping bag and his supply of vegetables. I looked at David as we eased our way down the mountain road.

"If he can handle this—then he's serious about the fight game."

Dave was busy staying on the road. Large mud holes from the spring thaw made the road almost impassable. "We could still get some snow up high where Tony's camped. I wonder if his clothes are warm enough."

The first night Tony was in the mountain camp, it snowed four inches. We imagined his reaction to the snow-covered ground when he climbed out of his tent. It would have been easy to give up and walk out of the mountains. There was nothing we could do but wait and see.

The following week, I drove back over to Roslyn and met Dave. We picked up some steaks and headed for the mountains. The roads had not improved and it took us two hours to cover the last ten miles. When we got to the campsite, the tent was still standing and Tony had built a small lean-to of tree branches. As we drove up, Tony crawled out of the tent. His hair was wild and a stubble of a beard made him look like a real mountain man.

"Man, you look like Grizzly Adams," I laughed.

"It's been snowing and the nights are cold, but I'm getting used to it." Tony sounded good.

Dave had brought out the steaks and a bottle of wine. "We came up to have dinner with you. Let's get a fire started." This time, Tony did a good job of building a fire. After we had eaten dinner, we sat around the camp fire and discussed Tony's future.

"I've started to run and I'm doing exercises. I can feel myself getting into shape. I know that in thirty days I'll be ready to get into some serious training. I'd like to get a fight scheduled as soon as possible."

When we drove out of the mountains, I had a good feeling about Tony's commitment. "We've got to figure a way to get some financial support for this guy, Dave. Without money the fight game is a tough nut to crack. I know some people in Oklahoma who might be willing to invest in his career.''

''The guy's really trying and I think he's a good person,'' Dave said. He had spent a lot of time with Tony, walking the hills and talking philosophy. I'd left an audio tape program and a player so Tony could become familiar with the concepts that had given me the tools to change my life.

My thoughts came back to the present.

I looked at Tony. The smoke in the visiting room was thick now and kids were running wildly, stumbling over chairs and people's feet. Mothers were hollering and occasionally a child would be slung over a knee and spanked in frustration. It's insane to live like this, I thought.

''You're at a point in your life, Tony, where you have to decide how you want to live. You've got the potential to be a tremendous fighter and a contributing member of society. But so did I when I was your age. I made the wrong decisions. You can be a big man in the 'big yard' and allow other people to control your life, or you can decide to make a commitment to yourself and become free to make your own decisions. It takes discipline and, for a period of time, it takes tremendous courage. You'll find many people who will try to pull you back and many temptations placed in front of you that will be hard to resist. You'll also discover that many people will accuse you of being a phoney and won't believe that you are sincere. But if you hang on, you'll find that gradually your life begins to work for you. I'll be with you when you appear before the parole board. If they release you, I'll provide as much support as possible, but whether you make it or not will depend on your own courage and commitment. You take care of yourself and keep your mind on what you want to do with your life.''

We stood up and shook hands. Tony's eyes met mine. ''I'm going to make it.''

He turned and I watched him walk back through the gates into the bowels of the prisons. My hopes were with Tony, and I could share with him some of the concepts that had helped me change. I could offer personal support and even try to arrange financial backing. But there were no guarantees. His fate was a question that he and time would have to answer.

The visiting room began to empty.

The Challenge
of Change

April 1, 1982. Cherry blossoms are just beginning to burst
around the Jefferson Memorial. Washington, D.C., is a beautiful city in the springtime. It's April Fool's Day and the
National Sheraton Hotel is full of conventions. Parties have
spilled out into the hallways, and the elevators are jammed
with neatly attired men and women, laughing and joking as
they hurry from party to party.

From the lounge on the sixteenth floor, you can look out
over the city and see the Washington Monument and the Pen-
tagon Building. The John F. Kennedy Center for the Performing Arts lies on the banks of the Potomac River. Washington,
D.C., is a city that inspires faith in the American tradition of
liberty and justice for all. The city was built on the belief that
change is possible and that negative backgrounds are
obstacles that can be overcome.

I'd flown to Washington, D.C., two days earlier. David Baker, correctional specialist for the Navy, had met me at the Sheraton for breakfast. David had been assigned to coordinate the production of a videotape training program I was producing at the Department of Defense Audio Visual Center. The program would be used by the Navy and Marine Corps as a vehicle to assist young men and women who were having difficulty adjusting to military life. David had been a counselor at the Monroe Reformatory in the fifties when I had been serving time.

It had been less than two years since Janie and I had decided to form the Human Development Training Institute. As I looked out over the nation's capitol, my thoughts ran back through the years. Where else but America? I thanked God for the gifts bestowed on me and reaffirmed my commitment to continue to assist people who were unable to see.

It was a long way from greasy fritters and six-wing. Life had been good to me. I was proud to be an American citizen — free to make my own choices, free to grow, willing to accept accountability for my own behavior. Freedom carries with it some heavy responsibilities.

The years that I spent locked in prison cells left scars and memories that will be with me to my death. Old fears and the burden of a prison record are never completely cancelled. I still approach security checks in airports cautiously, tiptoeing through the scanner, trying hard not to set off the alarm. I have changed, but change is difficult and takes continued effort and a willingness to handle set-backs in a constructive manner.

The idea that change was possible had come as a startling revelation to me. For many years I'd been locked in a mental prison stronger than steel bars or stone walls.

It was a prison like those that many of us gradually and incrementally build around ourselves, prisons that control our behavior and keep us from being the happy, productive people that we have the potential to become. I'd escaped from maximum security prisons, but escape from this mental prison took more courage and much more commitment.

The mental prisons can be built out of old attitudes that keep us from fully participating in life. They can be prisons of drugs or alcohol that warp our picture of reality and slowly eat away our dignity and self-esteem. The prisons that surround us take form through the way we think about ourselves, the information that we accept as the truth, the experiences we have and our reactions to them.

We start out in life with a blank canvas and then gradually begin to brush strokes on that canvas. The brushstrokes gradually paint a picture at the subconscious level of who we are and how we fit into our society. The first coat goes on and then another and then another until we have formed a self-image that controls our behavior. This happens not only to individuals, but also to teams, companies, and nations of people.

There was a period in history during which people operated upon and their behavior was controlled by an accepted truth—that the earth was flat. It took tremendous courage for someone in that environment to build some ships to sail around a "flat world." Can you imagine the reaction of most bankers if Christopher Columbus were seeking financial assistance for his journey? I'm sure the bankers' reaction would be, "Not with our money." Years ago, this single example set my head to spinning and caused a myriad of questions to suddenly surface. What are my flat worlds? Who says that I have to live in a prison, that I can't change? I suddenly discovered that I was living in my own flat world, created by information and experiences that I'd accepted, brushstrokes that had messed up my picture. How many of us are living in our own flat worlds?

There was a time in history when we had accepted the idea that a human could not run a mile in under four minutes. Then that barrier was broken, and in a short period of time, runners were breaking the four-minute barrier on a consistent basis. Where are our four-minute barriers? The barriers can be in our careers, in our sales quotas, in our families, in our social or recreational lives or in our spiritual lives. The first step toward lasting change is to recognize that we all have our own flat worlds and that they can be overcome.

How do we begin to break these mental barriers that hold us back and keep us from being happy, fulfilled human beings?

The answer lies within us. If the barriers are created by misin-
formation, as they were in Columbus' day, then we first need
to do some personal reflective thinking. Am I operating on
other people's opinions of who I am? Have I allowed my
current environment to control my picture of the truth? Has
peer pressure caused me to become involved in behavior that
will cause me lifelong difficulties?

Peer pressure in prisons causes young men and women to
develop habits and attitudes that keep them locked up. The
peer pressure on students in our schools can cause young
people to trap themselves in behavior that leads to pain and
unhappiness. Change can be very difficult under these
conditions.

One of life's truisms is that we move toward and become like
that which we think about. I discovered that when I stopped
thinking about doing wrong, it became less and less a part of
my behavior. As I began to discipline myself consciously to
think about what I wanted, I found that it became easier and
easier to function as a free, law-abiding citizen. For years I
had tried hard to control my behavior, giving no concern to
where I spent my time in my mind.

When things would go wrong, or I would have one too many
drinks, I'd find myself reverting to old behavioral patterns
that had kept me in trouble. As I began to make an effort to
discipline myself mentally, I found that I spent less and less
time thinking about stealing or other illegal activities.

Over the years, counselors and others have talked to me
about being accountable for my own behavior. They were
right about the need for accepting accountability, but I found
that accountability needs to begin with thoughts and then be
transferred to behavior. All meaningful and lasting change
starts first on the inside and then works its way out.

As I looked back at my life, I realized that I'd given up
accountability for most of my problems. When I was arrested
for a crime, I would fix the blame on the cops for patrolling
at the wrong time. Other times it would be my lawyer's or
the judge's fault. Eventually, we can fix the blame on society
for our problems. When I began to accept accountability for
my own life, the good as well as the bad, I began to get a

glimpse of what freedom is all about. I decided that if I didn't take control of my own behavior and operate within the guidelines of society, then someone would always be shaping me up and correcting me. When we accept accountability, life suddenly begins to work. There are still problems and setbacks, but we are able to manage them because we are in control.

I'd never realized the psychological power of goal setting until Lou Tice of The Pacific Institute had helped me understand it. We are all goal seeking by nature. I'd set the goal of getting out of prison and that goal controlled my behavior within the walls. But outside prison, I became like a ball in a pinball machine—moving towards whatever was currently dominant in my mind. As I looked back at my life, I was able to see where I'd allowed other people to set my goals. "Let's go get a drink." "Let's go rip this joint off." The decisions were based on emotions, not on my own desire to stay out of prison.

The awareness that we are only as strong and as consistent as our uppermost goal in life caused me to begin to question what was really of value to me. I'd always felt a certain emptiness even after I had become somewhat successful. Many people around me had strong spiritual goals. Most of the really consistent leaders I'd met had an uppermost goal that was spiritual. Spiritual concerns had always troubled me. Inside I knew that there was a God. The awareness that I'd some day need to come to grips with that aspect of life kept jogging my consciousness. Throughout my experiences both in and out of prison, I've struggled with the concepts of God, spirituality, and Christianity. It is a struggle that continues today. I constantly ask God for strength because I do accept the truth that God does exist. When I teach, I'm best when I've opened my mind and asked God to work through me. But there are still many unanswered questions.

Without a system of values, an organization will slowly lose productivity; without a moral code or a spiritual base, a nation will gradually move toward anarchy. Because God has gifted me with potential in the area of communication and leadership, it is my responsibility to use that potential, to be the best that I can be.

As stated earlier, the first step toward change is to begin to see that change is possible. Our awareness becomes limited through conditioning. We gradually get used to certain things in our lives. At first we may be bothered by being over-weight, but if we don't do something about our physical conditioning, we will get used to being heavy. The human being has within his or her brain a network of cells that operates very much like a filtering device. The network filters information. Two things will instantly get through this filter-ing device: (1) those things that are of value to us, and (2) those things that are a threat to us. One of our first questions must be, "What is of value to me?"

Another key factor in change is an understanding of self-image. Self-Image Psychology is based on the theory that you and I develop a self-image on the sub-conscious level. This self-image is created through our experiences and the informa-tion that we pick up in our environment. As we develop our self-image, we create a corresponding Comfort Zone, a place or set of places where we feel that we belong.

This Comfort Zone can be a neighborhood or a certain school. The military world can be a Comfort Zone. Whatever it is, when we get out of our Comfort Zone, our first tendency will be to get back to where we feel that we belong. Comfort Zones make change difficult because we sub-consciously work to get back to where we were before. To bring about lasting change, we must first understand Comfort Zones and then use the proper techniques to adjust to a new environment or social group.

In attempting to change or grow, we must also deal with old attitudes that may hold us back. Knowledge or information about emotional impact develops an attitude. Many of our current attitudes may be based on faulty or incomplete data. We can develop attitudes about places that we have never visited or attitudes about people we have never met. A young athlete explained his dislike for liver and onions (although he'd never eaten them) by telling me that neither his brothers and sisters nor his parents liked liver and onions. His attitude will keep him from trying this combination of foods. Our attitudes are created by our own perception of information and experiences. We interpret the experiences through our own "self-talk." As we listen to information, we talk to ourselves through our thoughts. What we record in the subconscious is how we feel and think about the information or experience. So this young athlete, listening to his parents, recorded that liver and onions were terrible. His negative attitude will cause him to avoid this dish. What are the negative attitudes that keep us from growth? How were they developed?

It is clear that our thoughts can become self-fulfilling prophecies, yet too often we neglect the power of this important factor in change. The self-talk just discussed either reinforces or will gradually modify our self-image. In bringing about lasting change, we must become conscious of what we think about. If we constantly think about drugs or alcohol, we will subconsciously seek out opportunities to use drugs and alcohol. If we always think about our weaknesses or our mistakes, we will recreate them in the future. An important concept in creating lasting change is to begin to monitor and discipline how we think. We have to think about what we think about.

The way we think also determines our motivation. If we are always thinking about what we don't want, it becomes difficult to motivate ourselves. If we begin to control what we think about and trigger pictures of what we want, we will create the drive and energy to accomplish the end result. If we want to get into physical condition, we must think about how good we will feel and look when we are in condition. Jogging, dieting and exercise are then clearly vehicles that lead us to the end result. Motivation should be like a child looking forward to Christmas or an adult looking forward to a vacation. To create constructive motivation and to begin to control our lives, we need to have predetermined worthwhile goals.

Once the goals have been determined, one of the keys to growth is practicing a skill or a behavior change that will move us toward the goal. Sometimes we are unable to find opportunities that allow us to practice often enough. There is a technique I have used for many years that speeds up the process of change. This technique is Constructive Synthetic Imagery. If you imagine yourself giving a lecture, it is recorded in your mind as though you have actually delivered your talk. This imagery and the words connected with it need to be in the first person present tense, as though you are standing in front of an audience.

The following steps demonstrate the use of Constructive Synthetic Imagery:

1. Design an affirmation (a statement of fact) that describes the attitude, behavior or skill as though you already possess it.

2. Read the words of the affirmation.

   I am a very effective public speaker and feel confident and poised in front of an audience.

3. See yourself performing the task or acting like you would like to be.

   I see myself in front of an audience, looking out at chairs filled with people leaning forward, listening to my presentation. As I imagine this, I see a podium and my hands and the faces of the audience.

4. Feel the emotion of being the kind of person you wish to be.

   I imagine the feeling of energy and excitement that comes from this experience. This emotion records.

5. Repeat the exercise as often as possible. I suggest twice a day: in the morning as you begin your day and in the evening as you end it. This will speed up the process dramatically.

   This exercise records a synthetic experience, and as I repeat the process daily, I gradually begin to feel confident and poised as I make a presentation to a group of people.

You can incorporate this process to bring about a change in attitude or to reach a goal. You must at the same time become conscious of your self-talk during the initial period of change. If you make a mistake during the period of change, don't spend time thinking about the mistake. Turn it loose and say to yourself, "The next time I intend to . . ." and trigger the picture of what you want to have happen. As you use this technique, express gratitude for the accomplishment of your goal when you first start the process. This is true belief without evidence — many refer to this quality as faith.

All of the above would not prove to be of significant value if we stopped there. The key to all meaningful and lasting change starts first on the inside and works its way out. We do not record our experiences, we record *how we feel* about those experiences. If every day we do things to the best of our ability, then all of our experiences record as successes. If we cheat or don't do our best, the our experiences have a negative feeling and they record as failures. Do your best and treat people as you would like to be treated and your life will begin to work for you. It's a simple message and yet I wasted thirty-seven years before I finally understood it.

> *"BUILD A BETTER WORLD,"* said God.
> And I answered,
> "HOW? THE WORLD IS SUCH A VAST PLACE,
> AND SO COMPLICATED NOW,
> AND I'M SMALL AND USELESS;
> THERE'S NOTHING I CAN DO."
> But God, in all His wisdom said,
> *"JUST BUILD A BETTER YOU."*